THE SPACES OF HOPE

Other books by Peter Jay

Poetry
LIFELINES
SHIFTING FRONTIERS

Translations
THE SONG OF SONGS

Ana Blandiana
THE HOUR OF SAND
with Anca Cristofovici

Ştefan Aug. Doinaş
ALIBI AND OTHER POEMS
with Virgil Nemoianu

Gérard de Nerval
THE CHIMERAS
with an essay by Richard Holmes

János Pilinszky
CRATER: POEMS 1974–75
CONVERSATIONS WITH SHERYL SUTTON
with Éva Major

Nichita Stănescu
THE STILL UNBORN ABOUT THE DEAD
with Petru Popescu

Editions
THE GREEK ANTHOLOGY
SAPPHO THROUGH ENGLISH POETRY
with Caroline Lewis

The Spaces of Hope

POETRY FOR OUR TIMES AND PLACES

Edited by Peter Jay

ANVIL PRESS POETRY

First published in 1998
by Anvil Press Poetry Ltd
Neptune House 70 Royal Hill London SE10 8RF

Selection and editorial matter © Peter Jay 1998

The acknowledgements page constitutes an extension of
the copyright page

ISBN 0 85646 301 9

This book is published with financial assistance from
The Arts Council of England

A catalogue record for this book
is available from the British Library

The moral rights of the editor have been asserted in
accordance with the Copyright, Designs and Patents Act 1988

Designed and set in Monotype Ehrhardt by Anvil
Printed and bound in England
by Alden Press, Osney Mead, Oxon.

FOR YOU

God knows what poetry is true
Among the pressing and the new,
God knows what poetry will last
Or how the stones of joy are cast.
The common thread, the common tongue
Binds all of us in speech and song:
Then if the casting of a spell
Sounds from these pages like a bell
Within your spirit, you have found
A space of hope on common ground.

ACKNOWLEDGEMENTS

All the poems in this book are copyrighted by their authors, represen-tatives and translators. They are from the publications listed in the Anvil Press Poetry bibliography on pages 211–218. We thank the poets, their representatives and translators for permission to reprint them here. All enquiries about rights should be addressed in the first instance to Anvil Press, except for the poems listed below, where they should be addressed to their publisher.

We thank Carcanet Press Ltd for permission to include 'The Magi' and 'The Undertaking' by Louise Glück from *The First Five Books of Poems* (1997), copyright © Louise Glück 1997; Edwin Morgan's trans-lation of 'Coolie' by Sándor Weöres, from *Collected Translations* (1996), copyright © Edwin Morgan 1996; and 'The Moonflower' and 'The Question' by F.T. Prince, from *Collected Poems* (1993), copyright © F.T. Prince 1993.

Contents

Foreword

This anthology celebrates thirty years of publishing contemporary poetry and poetry in translation. The thread that binds the selection is simply that I have, at one time or another, published in book form all the poems in this collection. With two exceptions, they come from the titles which are listed in the bibliography. The first is the late Anne Pennington's single poem, which emerged among the drafts of translations that formed the bulk of her papers. The second is Joe Winter's four-line poem which has stayed in my head ever since I printed it in 1966 in *New Measure*, the poetry magazine which I edited as a student and from which grew the idea of starting a poetry publishing house.

The artistic impulse is essentially generous and optimistic, otherwise in the face of death there would be no point in making a work of art. Though its subject-matter sometimes seems to spring more from human misery than human joy, good poetry always comes from close engagement with and delight in humanity's common and linking faculty, language. This it has in common with song, as the survival of the term 'lyric' to describe a common kind of poem testifies.

Still it has surprised me – since I had no predetermined plan when beginning to shape this book – that this collection of largely contemporary poems should so naturally assemble itself with such a robust tendency towards hope and joy. Among many other poems, those by Ivan V. Lalić, whose work I have loved since it was first recommended to me by Anne Pennington in 1979, and who through the title of the book is its presiding spirit, express those qualities memorably.

Memorability has been a strong criterion in my selection. I have never been good at picking up verse by heart; but good poetry leaves a distinct impress on one's memory. It has an unmistakeable tone or aura: you often go back to a poem because you want to recall its exact phrasing and refresh your memory. These are poems I keep going back to, poems which have in various ways proved themselves durable.

Many people find translated poetry off-putting or problematic and deny themselves the pleasure of reading translations because they are not quite sure what they are dealing with. To such readers I would say, just read the English as it is. A translated poem is offered as an English poem and must stand or fall as such. Do not worry about what is supposedly lost in translation: concentrate rather on what is gained by it. I count myself fortunate to publish some exceptional poet-translators; their work is definitely among my favourite modern poetry in English. I should perhaps add that the close reading involved in translating a poet is so similar to the editorial process that, having had the opportunity to combine translation with editing and publishing some poets whose work has meant a greal deal to me, I feel no need to apologize for including some of their and my work.

I decided to give translators' names in italics below the name of the original poet, without the customary prefix of 'translated by'. This is partly to avoid the tedium of repetition, and partly, too, to sidestep the question of different kinds of translation. (This book contains examples of straightforward translation, of freer versions, imitations or adaptations, and of poems which are simply inspired by, or which take the original poem as a starting-point.) But it is also to make a point. Poets who make translations are secondary authors in one sense, but they are the primary authors of the English that you read under some-one else's name, and this deserves assertion. Just as the national life of Britain has been continually varied and invigorated by immigration, so our literature, especially our poetry, has been enriched by diverse kinds of translation from Chaucer onwards.

I should like to thank Emma Cooney, Jaimy Deol, Tatiana Schenk, Bill Swainson and Kit Yee Wong for their help in the preparation of this book; and record my gratitude to the poets for their inspiriting work.

PETER JAY
Greenwich, October 1998

The Spaces of Hope

'Could it be true'

Could it be true we live on earth?
On earth forever?

Just one brief instant here.

Even the finest stones begin to split,
even gold is tarnished,
even precious bird-plumes
shrivel like a cough.

Just one brief instant here.

NEZAHUALCOYOTL
Edward Kissam and Michael Schmidt

A Chance

The rest you know. My job was simply
to bring you this far. Now you'll all start
talking at once, and then the hero's
corpse in the labyrinth, and the chord,
the brass band striking up for the march,
the silence that follows, and the still
profounder silence that will answer, –
all these will be trampled underfoot.
But my job was only to bring you
this far – and that's all. Now: there's a chance
for the majority of you. True,
only a single chance. But it's there!

ŞTEFAN AUG. DOINAŞ
Peter Jay and Virgil Nemoianu

Childhood

TO ROBERT WELLS

Imperceptible, at sunrise, the slight
Breeze stirs the dreaming boy, till silently
He edges free from sleep and takes the kite,
Huge on his shoulders like an angel's wings,
To climb the hill beyond the drowsing city.
Released, the first ungainly waverings

Are guided out, above the still valley,
Constrained to one smooth flow, diminishing
Until the pacing boy can hardly see
The dark dot shift against the constant blue:
He squats and stares: in his hand the taut string
Tugs, strains – as if there were still more to do.

DICK DAVIS

A Picture

FOR TIANTIAN'S FIFTH BIRTHDAY

Morning arrives in a sleeveless dress
apples tumble all over the earth
my daughter is drawing a picture
how vast is a five-year-old sky
your name has two windows
one opens towards a sun with no clock-hands
the other opens towards your father
who has become a hedgehog in exile
taking with him a few unintelligible characters
and a bright red apple
he has left your painting
how vast is a five-year-old sky

BEI DAO
Bonnie S. McDougall

On the Death of Friends in Childhood

We shall not ever meet them bearded in heaven,
Nor sunning themselves among the bald of hell;
If anywhere, in the deserted schoolyard at twilight,
Forming a ring, perhaps, or joining hands
In games whose very names we have forgotten.
Come, memory, let us seek them there in the shadows.

DONALD JUSTICE

'A little girl...'

A little girl sees her granny spinning.
She wants a hank of flax for her doll
and bides her time.
There! Granny's nodding off,
so she steals up, pulls
a strand as the bobbin spins,
and triumphant skips away
with some wool dyed saffron gold –
about as much as a bird would take
building its nest.

VICTOR HUGO
Harry Guest

His Dream

I am a child, a child, a child.
This afternoon is huge and very still.
I hide among the tall white weeds;
the sky rests on their tips.
The air is heavy, as thick as bees

19

that swarmed once on the wall
and we weren't scared and the bees
stayed a while and went on.
I cannot hear my friends, looking for me
far away. The ground is rich
and one by one small creatures
come toward me. I understand.
The world waits on my breath:
there is time for anything.

PHILIP HOLMES

The Skeleton Dance

We went to the pictures one bright afternoon,
There were serials, slapstick, and then a cartoon
Of skeletons dancing. That night I was soon
Woken up by the skeleton dance.

Those skeletons jiggled their fingers and toes
And juggled their thigh bones and skulls with no nose,
They grinned as their eye sockets gaped, and I froze
At the clattering skeletons' dance.

I ran to my mother and shook her awake –
'It's those skeletons dancing!' 'Those what? For my sake
Get back to your bed, it's past midnight, why make
Such a fuss for a skeleton dance!'

I said I was sorry, I pushed back her hair
To kiss her smooth forehead, now shining and bare,
And saw that her skin hid a skull. Even here
Was a skeleton waiting to dance.

Since that night long ago I have tried not to see
Her forehead – or yours – for it's bound to show me
The bone just below, which is waiting to be
Whirled away in the skeleton dance.

RUTH SILCOCK

Young Girl Sulking

To think that she couldn't be something else – anything else.
    Opposite her
that invisible mirror, looking at itself, seeing
her motion before she moved. And outside, in the garden,
her girl friends calling to her, skipping rope,
swinging under the trees, covering their breasts,
armpits, hair, with lemon blossoms. She, as though not
    hearing,
stitched away with the giant, archaic sewing machine, in the
    room,
stitched hard, almost violently: cold white sheets for a bridal
    bed.
And opposite, the mirror showed her over and over again that
    she was beautiful.

YANNIS RITSOS
Edmund Keeley

A Childhood Recollection
EARLY TWENTIES

I once had an aunt who raved about Blackheath
though my parents mocked her when she was gone

but I was a boy whose heart had ears
and knowing that words were more than words

her words survived their edge of scorn
and Blackheath grew on the rim of the world,

and Blackheath grew on the rim of the world
with white houses in a white field

with oceans of room, and starched lawns
and grand, inscrutable, far views –

with oceans of room engulfed in silence
the slow horses turning eyes –

oceans of room, and church spires
to balance the distance, tight and smooth –

with oceans of room engulfed in silence
to endure all the scorn in the world.

DONALD WARD

A Photograph of Two Brothers

How old were we? Eight, ten or so?
I seem the tearful one – you glow,
All bounce and boyish confidence,
Which looking back now makes no sense.
I haven't changed that much – and yes,
I hurt too easily I guess,
Though mostly now the tears I shed
Are proxy tears, for you, long dead.

DICK DAVIS

Fingers in the Door

FOR KATE

Careless for an instant I closed my child's fingers in the jamb.
    She
Held her breath, contorted the whole of her being, foetus-
    wise, against the
Burning fact of the pain. And for a moment
I wished myself dispersed in a hundred thousand pieces
Among the dead bright stars. The child's cry broke,
She clung to me, and it crowded in to me how she and I were
Light-years from any mutual help or comfort. For her I cast
    seed
Into her mother's womb; cells grew and launched itself as a
    being:
Nothing restores her to my being, or ours, even to the mother
    who within her
Carried and quickened, bore, and sobbed at her separation,
    despite all my envy,
Nothing can restore. She, I, mother, sister, dwell dispersed
    among dead bright stars:
We are there in our hundred thousand pieces!

DAVID HOLBROOK

Ghazal of the Dead Child

Every afternoon in Granada,
every afternoon a child dies.
Every afternoon the water sits down
to converse with its friends.

The dead wear wings of moss.
The clouded wind and clean wind
are two pheasants that fly around the towers
and the day is a wounded boy.

No blade of lark remained in the air
when I found you in the wine caverns.
No crumb of cloud remained on the earth
when you were drowning in the river.

A giant of water fell upon the hills
and the valley went tumbling, with dogs and iris.
Your body, in the violet shadow of my hands,
dead on the bank, was an archangel of cold.

FEDERICO GARCÍA LORCA
Christopher Maurer

The File

Words cross the road
Like a file of orphans
From the Children's Home,
Each with a fist clenched
On the coat of the one in front,
Their only care
Not to be cut off
One from another.

ANA BLANDIANA
Peter Jay and Anca Cristofovici

Mr Wathen's Demise

When in wartime the prep-school head changed my Jewish
    surname
because it sounded German,
we did not question his decision.

That headmaster has long since met his end.
His next-in-line but two or three
pointed to the old man's full-length portrait
and told me how this happened.

Mr W raised his brolly and strode
confidently into the Finchley Road.

Like Moses crossing the Red Sea, I thought.

DANIEL WEISSBORT

Proofs

Death will not correct
a single line of verse
she is no proof-reader
she is no sympathetic
lady editor

a bad metaphor is immortal

a shoddy poet who has died
is a shoddy dead poet

a bore bores after death
a fool keeps up his foolish chatter
from beyond the grave

TADEUSZ RÓŻEWICZ
Adam Czerniawski

T. Sturge Moore

When I was young
I found T. Sturge Moore
a very boring poet –
but now that I am old
I find him even more boring still.

GAVIN EWART

Someone

someone is dressing up for death today, a change of skirt or tie
eating a final feast of buttered sliced pan, tea
scarcely having noticed the erection that was his last
shaving his face to marble for the icy laying out
spraying with deodorant her coarse armpit grass
someone today is leaving home on business
saluting, terminally, the neighbours who will join in the cortège
someone is trimming his nails for the last time, a precious
      moment
someone's thighs will not be streaked with elastic in the future
someone is putting out milkbottles for a day that will not come
someone's fresh breath is about to be taken clean away
someone is writing a cheque that will be marked 'drawer deceased'
someone is circling posthumous dates on a calendar
someone is listening to an irrelevant weather forecast
someone is making rash promises to friends
someone's coffin is being sanded, laminated, shined
who feels this morning quite as well as ever
someone if asked would find nothing remarkable in today's date
perfume and goodbyes her final will and testament
someone today is seeing the world for the last time
as innocently as he had seen it first

DENNIS O'DRISCOLL

ASPEN TREE, your leaves glance white into the dark.
My mother's hair was never white.

Dandelion, so green is the Ukraine.
My yellow-haired mother did not come home.

Rain cloud, above the well do you hover?
My quiet mother weeps for everyone.

Round star, you wind the golden loop.
My mother's heart was ripped by lead.

Oaken door, who lifted you off your hinges?
My gentle mother cannot return.

PAUL CELAN
Michael Hamburger

Paul Celan

Shut inside this rotating
ghost-house, life,
with little openings each
giving on
its own reality
– we live,
are at home here –
most of us gather
at the biggest one,
this is the world,
we say.

At yours
sat
only you –

eye black
diamond,
heart
a bloodstone.

OLAV H. HAUGE
Robin Fulton

At the Window

I think of the dead who were buried today,
Of those hurried away
Without time for the painful farewells,
And of those who have waited so long
(Whether waiting for birth or death,
The waiting is long).

And the strangeness of making a journey
Without the removal van,
And the unfamiliar landscape, where time
Rolls backwards and forwards,
And the mind tossed over earth's shoulder
Clutches the last known thing.

And I look at the steady stare of the sky
And my cat stretched languidly out,
I think of the dead walking naked about,
How it feels in a mansion of mirrors
To open a door.

HEATHER BUCK

After Death

They say Death's perfect Peace and Rest. That's interesting.
But if we don't have consciousness, how shall we know we're
    resting?

GAVIN EWART

Villon on Death

FOR BASIL BUNTING

POETRY TO GO
that's what
    Villon bought
at the hot dog
    stand
        the sleek hot dogs not so hot
        blotched thighs round a worn twat

Death. Margot
    sans linen
kept one wolf warm
    when the pack ran
through the streets
    outside her kitchen
in the cold season,
    I,
Francis Villon
    clerk, poet
who lived by
    the short dagger
hung
    mid-stomach
between shanks.
    No engine cranks

the restless tongue
	the nicked lip.
Montfaucon
	temporal exit
from the death pit.
	The last jack-off
free
	on the city
gibbet,
	the turnip topped
galvanic in death
	the jack-rabbit.

PETER WHIGHAM

'Think of your conception'

Think of your conception, you'll soon forget
what Plato puffs you up with, all that
'immortality' and 'divine life' stuff.

*Man, why dost thou think of Heaven? Nay
consider thine origins in common clay*

's one way of putting it but not blunt enough.

Think of your father, sweating, drooling, drunk,
you, his spark of lust, his spurt of spunk.

PALLADAS
Tony Harrison

Dead Language

He with the beating wings
outside who brushes the door,
that is your brother, you hear him.
Laurio he says, water,
a bow, colourless, deep.

He came down with the river,
drifting around mussel
and snail, spread like a fan
on the sand and was green.

Warne he says and *wittan*,
the crow has no tree,
I have the power to kiss you,
I dwell in your ear.

Tell him you do not
want to listen –
he comes, an otter, he comes
swarming like hornets, he cries,
a cricket, he grows with the marsh
under your house, he whispers
in the well, *smordis* you hear,
your black alder will wither,
and die at the fence tomorrow.

JOHANNES BOBROWSKI
Ruth & Matthew Mead

Slowly the Truth Dawns

To waken, and feel
your heart sink
heavy and dark

and hardening…
Slowly the sea lifts its billow,
slowly the forest reddens in the gorge,
slowly the flames begin to lick in hell,
slowly the truth dawns.

OLAV H. HAUGE
Robin Fulton

Something Like a Sky

Something in us has suddenly cleared.
Like a sky.
Like a still-life, alive.
Behind us, our footsteps and voices.
Beyond the walls, a wide silence.
The air is white and open, ready for snow.

ROBIN FULTON

The Diver

TO MICHAELIS NICOLETSÉAS

The blue-cold spasm passes,
And he's broken in.
Assailed by silence he descends
Lost suddenly

To air and sunburned friends,
And wholly underwater now
He plies his strength against
The element that

Slows all probings to their feint.
Still down, till losing
Light he drifts to the wealthy wreck
And its shade-mariners

Who flit about a fractured deck
That holds old purposes
In darkness. He hesitates, then
Wreathes his body in.

DICK DAVIS

Iphigenia of Bochum

In the midst of this breathless epoch
in the panorama of shrapnel-scarred asphalt
antiquity a little careworn, cool jazz
and lilac smile of filmstars
in the midst of neon-pale prosperity
confronting bar-sniggers and newspapers
here among thieves and accountants
as inspiring as buried cries
in the ruins: a face
a brow, almost unravaged
Iphigenia of Bochum.

Troy and Thule in the grey eyes
eyes which made submachineguns
useless, eyes which kissed the hunted moon
through the military hospital window
when no air-raid warning fell from the sky
eyes, knowing, stirring imagination
eyes like symbols: a cross deep
in the iris and the small yearning
for avenues where there was perhaps

a last gesture: Hector went
columns of tanks. Gone.

On the lips the forgotten song
lovely desire and the question
for which there is no new word as yet
lips carved in steel, prelude
taken up by the curve of the hips
a theme for Bach, with the grace
of French goddesses
lips of timeless love –
But too fleetingly touched
but too purely desired:
Iphigenia of Bochum.

HEINZ WINFRIED SABAIS
Ruth & Matthew Mead

The Haunting

I see you profiled in the window of a bus,
Or in a queue, your smile on someone else's face.

You are what might have been, a spirit from the past.
At night I hold you in my dreams and lay your ghost.

JAMES HARPUR

Sentence

Whenever sentence is passed
a great darkness falls
on the courtroom
as during crucifixion.

But now, in mid–October,
light's candle
burns with bright flame
about your face.

The dried-up palette
of distant gardens,
false witness against the painter
who has gone away for a moment, no one knows where.

Before I realized it
judgement was passed
on love:
sentenced for life.

ANTONÍN BARTUŠEK
Ewald Osers

Sixth Elegy

APHASIA

I stand between two idols and cannot choose
either, I stand between
two idols, and it is raining thinly
and I cannot choose either,
and waiting in the thin rain the idols
turn into wood. I stand
and cannot choose between the two
pieces of wood, and it rains thinly, I cannot
choose in the putrid rain. I stand
and the two wooden pieces display
their ribs whitened by the thin rain.
I stand between two horse-skeletons
and cannot choose either, I stand
and it is raining thinly, melting the earth

under the white bones, and I cannot choose.
I stand between two pits, and it rains thinly
and the water gnaws at the earth
with the teeth of a starved rat.
I stand between two pits, shovel in hand
and cannot, in the thin rain
choose which I should fill up first
with the earth bitten by the thin rain.

NICHITA STĂNESCU
Peter Jay and Petru Popescu

Up Through the River Valley

I step upwards lightly on the stones,
fresh rivery gust against me,
and I sing.
Sorrow is the well of strength,
the glaciers weep in the sun,
why do I go more lightly
against than with?

OLAV H. HAUGE
Robin Fulton

Here in Katmandu

We have climbed the mountain.
There's nothing more to do.
It is terrible to come down
To the valley
Where, amidst many flowers,
One thinks of snow,

As, formerly, amidst snow,
Climbing the mountain,
One thought of flowers,
Tremulous, ruddy with dew,
In the valley.
One caught their scent coming down.

It is difficult to adjust, once down,
To the absence of snow.
Clear days, from the valley,
One looks up at the mountain.
What else is there to do?
Prayer wheels, flowers!

Let the flowers
Fade, the prayer wheels run down.
What have these to do
With us who have stood atop the snow
Atop the mountain,
Flags seen from the valley?

It might be possible to live in the valley,
To bury oneself among flowers,
If one could forget the mountain,
How, never once looking down,
Stiff, blinded with snow,
One knew what to do.

Meanwhile it is not easy here in Katmandu,
Especially when to the valley
That wind which means snow
Elsewhere, but here means flowers,
Comes down,
As soon it must, from the mountain.

DONALD JUSTICE

The Undertaking

The darkness lifts, imagine, in your lifetime.
There you are – cased in clean bark you drift
through weaving rushes, fields flooded with cotton.
You are free. The river films with lilies,
shrubs appear, shoots thicken into palm. And now
all fear gives way: the light
looks after you, you feel the waves' goodwill
as arms widen over the water; Love,

the key is turned. Extend yourself –
it is the Nile, the sun is shining,
everywhere you turn is luck.

LOUISE GLÜCK

Dust

Into the empty spaces comes Wednesday
offering itself like a virgin,
as if I didn't know how to please
or as if the sky had fallen in,
showering me with kisses.

I peel a wet petal from the bark,
let the rain drum its future into me.
It tells longings like beads, Ariadne
sliding through them in knots.

Her necklace is private as a fan,
to be cast aground with other common things.
One day you will taste it in leaf
or in the not–quite–ready autumn plums,

the dust on their purple sheen
like the gathering of souls.

SUE STEWART

The Heart of the Quartz Pebble

They played with the pebble
The stone like any other stone
Played with them as if it had no heart

They got angry with the pebble
Smashed it in the grass
Puzzled they saw its heart

They opened the pebble's heart
In the heart a snake
A sleeping coil without dreams

They roused the snake
The snake shot up into the heights
They ran off far away

They looked from afar
The snake coiled round the horizon
Swallowed it like an egg

They came back to the place of their game
No trace of snake or grass or bits of pebble
Nothing anywhere far around

They looked at each other they smiled
And they winked at each other

VASKO POPA
Anne Pennington

Everything in the City

Everything in the city comes to this table.
There must be something to be said about these
Explosions of laughter at the stairhead,
Rumours of approach in the tunnels.
Water is scattered in the air, everywhere
Attesting to the importance of clouds
And the weather changes every few hours
Where blind men are making journeys over the city
Tapping trees and observing the shadow
Sound casts. Processions are crossing it
Bearing advertisements.
Essential oils fry in the pan: 'Bury it in
An inch of water, it will sing for five minutes.'
Everything in the city comes to this table.

JOHN WELCH

No Half-Measures

As for me, I have my daily wage, he said. Forget the others.
I took a nail out of the wall, looked through the hole,
glued the glass pane with flour-and-water paste, smoked a
    cigarette.
I took the garbage can down to the curb
along with the cardboard box full of orange peels.
I combed my hair carefully, shined my shoes with spit,
ran a wet towel under my armpits,
stood at the window thinking. I spoke inside myself.
I'm ready now, ready at any moment – he says –
to present myself to the florist, the surgeon, or the prosecutor.

YANNIS RITSOS   *Athens, 20 January 1972*
Edmund Keeley

'Bring wine, my boy'

Bring wine, my boy – I'm dying now I know,
Blind-drunk is how I'll quit this earthly show;
I entered life completely ignorant
And that's precisely how I plan to go.

FAGHANI
Dick Davis

A Remarkable Thing

A remarkable thing about wine,
which we drunkards and lechers all bless so,
is the way it makes girls look more fine –
but ourselves, on the contrary, less so.

GAVIN EWART

'A pattern of birds'
from LOVE POEMS OF THE VITH DALAI LAMA

A pattern of birds,
    crossed twigs,
& the last milestone
    have brought love
like luck
    to these two
met
    in this hedge-tavern,
where an old woman
    ladles out wine to them.

She will go on
    serving wine
on the periphery
    of their lives
at parting,
    at welcoming,
at childbirth.

PETER WHIGHAM

'Drunk with Mine Host and the Fiddlers'
(FLORIO'S MONTAIGNE)

Drunk with mine host and the fiddlers,
I will not home tonight.
Let the cat yawn on the window-ledge
Until the stars go out;
The bed can gape and lie hungry –
I'm fed with wine for a change
And music, out of range of the house
Where the spider I call habit
Spins my history tight.
I am breathing this other air
Like gas, gratefully, while the strings
Modulate to the dark
Advantage of the heart.

Here drunk with mine host and the fiddlers
I lose the route hither and hence,
Alone in the turbulence
As the fisherman frees himself
And the fish by discarding the net,
Standing erect in the prow,

At ease in the present air
As never at sea before,
In earnest, as if never again.

MICHAEL SCHMIDT

Waiting

Every word is a jar
Almost full of alcohol:
Some drink it;
Some disinfect their wounds with it;
Others shake it in the light and cloud it,
Making the dregs and silt rise;
Some line the flagons up
In the order of their size,
Playing soldiers with them;
Some group them
By colours, or by shapes;
Others uncork them
To release the alcohol
Or to try it out amazed
Setting it alight.

I don't do anything.
I sit and wait
To remind myself
Of the fruit
From which I distilled it.
What was it like?

ANA BLANDIANA
Peter Jay and Anca Cristofovici

Something Said, Waking Drunk on a Spring Day

It's like boundless dream here in this
world, nothing anywhere to trouble us.

I have, therefore, been drunk all day,
a shambles of sleep on the front porch.

Coming to, I look into the courtyard.
There's a bird among blossoms calling,

and when I ask what season this is,
an oriole's voice drifts on spring winds.

Overcome, verging on sorrow and lament,
I pour another drink. Soon, awaiting

this bright moon, I'm chanting a song.
And now it's over, I've forgotten why.

LI PO
David Hinton

Prayer

Give me a death like Buddha's. Let me fall
over from eating mushrooms Provençal,
a peasant wine pouring down my shirt-front,
my last request not a cry but a grunt.
Kicking my heels to heaven, may I succumb
tumbling into a rosebush after a love
half my age. Though I'm deposed, my tomb
shall not be empty, may my belly show above
my coffin like a distant hill, my mourners come

as if to pass an hour in the country,
to see the green, that old anarchy.

STANLEY MOSS

'On Aspalathoi...'

Sounion was lovely that spring day –
the Feast of the Annunciation.
Sparse green leaves around rust-coloured stone,
red earth, and aspalathoi
with their huge thorns and their yellow flowers
already out.
In the distance the ancient columns, strings of a harp still
    vibrating...

Peace.
– What could have made me think of Ardiaios?
Possibly a word in Plato, buried in the mind's furrows:
the name of the yellow bush
hasn't changed since his time.
That evening I found the passage:
'They bound him hand and foot,' it says,
'they flung him down and flayed him,
they dragged him along
gashing his flesh on thorny aspalathoi,
and they went and threw him into Tartarus, torn to shreds.'
In this way Ardiaios, the terrible Pamphylian tyrant,
paid for his crimes in the nether world.

GEORGE SEFERIS   *31 March 1971*
Edmund Keeley and Philip Sherrard

Étude

Buttercup, cowslip, dandelion, chamomile –
Each tiny yellow flower reminds me of joy,
The unreasoned joy often found with hope,
Like the fine embroidery on her blouse, perhaps,
If one could imagine hope in a blouse.
Translated into the tongue of music,
Tiny yellow flowers (buttercup, cowslip…)
Would ring in C major. As spring nears its end
There are fields where oil-to-be blooms
Thick, bright-yellow, in tiny flowers,
Breathing happiness into the blue. Unreasoned.

Between the leaves of a palimpsest of your years
And mine, my love, I have discovered
Traces of tiny yellow flowers between the lines
Describing the places we love: hope, your little
Sister, has been playing with our book.

IVAN V. LALIĆ
Francis R. Jones

Peach Blossom

In rain it opens, and falls in wind.
How many days can we see the peach blossom?

This brevity is in the blossom's nature:
Not that the wind has been guilty, or the rain kind.

YI KI
Kim Jong-gil

Don't Talk to Me about Bread

she kneads
deep into the night
and the whey-coloured dough

springy and easy and yielding to her will

is revenge. Like a rival,
dough toys with her. Black-brown hands in the belly
bringing forth a sigh.

She slaps it, slaps it double with fists
with heel of hand applies the punishment
not meant for bread

and the bitch on the table sighs
and exhales a little spray of flour
a satisfied breath of white

on her hand

mocking the colour
robbing hands of their power
as they go through the motions, kneading...
She listens for the sigh which haunts

from the wrong side of her own door
from this wanton cheat of dough
this whey-faced bitch rising up

in spite of her fight, rising up
her nipples, her belly, rising up
two legs, dear god, in a blackwoman's rage...

Laughing at her, all laughing at her:
giggling bitch, abandoned house, and Man
still promising from afar what men promise...

Hands come to life again: knife
in the hand, the belly ripped open, and she smears

white lard and butter, she sprinkles
a little obeah of flour and curses to stop up the wound.

Then she doubles the bitch up
with cuffs, wrings her like washing
till she's the wrong shape

and the tramp lets out a damp, little sigh
a little hiss of white
enjoying it.

E.A. MARKHAM

Riddle

I have heard of something hatched in a corner:
It thrusts, rustles, raises its hat
A bride grabbed at that boneless thing,
Handled it proudly: a prince's daughter
Covered that swelling creature with her robe.

ANONYMOUS OLD ENGLISH
Michael Alexander

Black Beans

Afternoons I pick a book up
Afternoons I put a book down
Afternoons it occurs to me there is war
Afternoons I forget each and every war
Afternoons I grind coffee
Afternoons I put the ground-up coffee
Together again backwards lovely
Black beans
Afternoons I get dressed undressed
First put on make-up then I wash myself
Sing am silent

SARAH KIRSCH
Margitt Lehbert

A Dull Morning Enlivened

On a dull morning
a student brings me a poem
comparing her husband's cock to an aubergine.
I think: this is more like it!

GAVIN EWART

Bacon and Cabbage

He said that it was a fact.
The whole field to be turned
into a small village
with our own roads, post-office,
sweetshop to include toys.
No adults.

Their heads wouldn't get in the doors.
Brothers and sisters would live together
and never go off to get married.
The boys would go fishing
and the girls could come too,
if they didn't want to stay behind
baking apple tarts. There would be no more bacon and cabbage.
No one would stand for it.
Connemara ponies would do all the work
it would only take an hour a week.
I only had to send in my order
and my bed would be teeming with pups.
When I asked was it really really a fact,
he shouted. Had I not heard the priest
announce it off the altar on Sunday?
I hadn't because I never listened anyway.
But I couldn't believe
that Father O'Shea would make such final remarks
about bacon and cabbage.

MARTINA EVANS

Too Many Cooks

My fingers stretch the yeast.
It's fresh and suggestive,
slides down the cup's hill – kitchen's
warm, and the bowl. Hands are cool.

Sugar grains fly like spore,
white on cream. The jug tilts,
its warm water a spilt pool.
In it falls my wooden spoon.

Flour and salt marry:
one is vague, one pragmatic.
Liquid foams at the cup's lip –
flour invites it, yeast carries.

The towel has discretion,
I use it as duvet
while boasting hours pass below.
Dough settles for the bowl's rim.

My punch deflates. I lift
and knead for eight minutes,
forcing in gobbets of air:
plop in a tin, brush with egg.

Poppy seeds hurtle down.
Somewhere in their tight heads
is a harvest, a red past.
I cover them with darkness.

Our dough grows outlandish,
meets the oven's burnt truth
and comes out terracotta –
Vesuvian, fixed in mid-

SUE STEWART

Vesuvius, 24 August AD 79

The vine-leaf once cast green shadows here,
    yearly the vine-tubs dripped with the god's grapes;
Bacchus was at home in these hills; fauns and his goat-men
    danced on their slopes; the place was holy
To *Hercules*, and *Venus* was happier here
    than ever in her own *Lacedaemon*.

Today, flame & mournful lava have drowned all that there was.
And the gods themselves murmur at the force of their own
    doom.

MARTIAL
Peter Whigham

Hölderlin in Tübingen

Trees, earthly, and light
in which the boat stands, called,
the oar against the bank, the lovely
slope, before this door
walked the shadow which has
fallen upon a river
Neckar, which was green, Neckar,
winding through
meadows and willows.

Tower,
that it be dwelt in
like a day, the walls'
weight, the weight
against the green,
trees and water, to weigh
both in one hand:
the bell sounds down
over the roofs, the clock
moves to the turn
of the weathervane.

JOHANNES BOBROWSKI
Ruth & Matthew Mead

Half of Life

With yellow pears hangs down
And full of wild roses
The land into the lake,
You loving swans,
And drunk with kisses
You dip your heads
Into water, the holy-and-sober.

But oh, where shall I find
When winter comes, the flowers, and where
The sunshine
And shade of the earth?
The walls loom
Speechless and cold, in the wind
Weathercocks clatter.

FRIEDRICH HÖLDERLIN
Michael Hamburger

Corycian Saffron

They smell of *Corycian* saffron, of a
    girl's tooth biting a fresh apple,
Of first bunches of white grapes & sheep-cropped
    grass & myrtle leaves & chafed amber.
They're in the herb harvest. They're in the flame
    golden with myrrh. Earth smells of them
In summer after rain, and jewelry
    reeking of expensive heads.
Your kisses, my cold jewel, smell thus. How would
    they smell if love had warmed their giving?

MARTIAL
Peter Whigham

The Moonflower

The secret drops of love run through my mind:
Midnight is filled with sounds of the full sea
That has risen softly among the rocks;
Air stirs the cedar tree.

Somewhere a fainting sweetness is distilled.
It is the moonflower hanging in its tent
Of twisted broad-leaved branches by the stony path
That squanders the cool scent.

Pallid, long as a lily, it swings a little
As if drunk with its own perfume and the night,
Which draws its perfume out and leaves the flower
The weaker for its flight.

Detached from my desires, in an oblivion
Of this world that surrounds me, in weariness
Of all but darkness, silence, starry solitude
I too feel that caress –

Delicate, serene and lonely, peaceful, strange
To the intellect and the imagination,
The touch with which reality wounds and ravishes
Our inmost desolation.

All being like the moonflower is dissatisfied
For the dark kiss that the night only gives,
And night gives only to the soul that waits in longing,
And in that only lives.

F.T. PRINCE

A Picture of R.C. in a Prospect of Blossom

In the still, warm air of afternoon
you stand beneath the magnolia tree
watching the blossoms fall. Your face
upturned is secret as the moon,
bland in the blue, though hours too soon.
A petal descends with deathly grace,
another lies on your arm, I see.

It is your eleventh spring, and yet
your first – because you feel it so:
never before such scents to smell,
never such drenching slippery sweat,
such birdsong, or such flowers to pet.
You run from the house (whose wintry spell
still mutters of storms and ice and snow)

to skip barefooted on the grass,
or jump from favourite stone to stone,
or else sit solemn on the stoop
watching the link-arm lovers pass –
as if they held some magic glass
in which came shimmering into shape
scenes of your future fully grown.

And now what silent reverie
holds you with bated thought and breath
beneath the surprising moon, among
the flakes of blossom still breaking free
and the fallen abundance of the tree?
I see you only statue-strong
and tiptoe-deep in brilliant death.

TONY CONNOR

Mirages

They smile at us from last summer,
Bowls of remembered roses,
First-class journeys through England.

Other voyages are contemplated,
Steam-shrouded coastlines
Dancing on the horizon – always towards.

Cruel quarantine of the self-renewing art,
Line by line it commemorates itself,
Turns out drawers, stitches the tattered coat.

Dreams depress, bedding us in soil
Soft as persuasion, deeper than eiderdowns,
Beyond earshot of the conscientious spade.

Soon it will be time for the glad
Pick to smite the embittered ice.
Mirror or mirage, the perspective is the same.

MARCUS CUMBERLEGE

The Rose

Such concentration on a single rose,
you look as though you watch it breathe the scent
till I am watching you and held intent,
your breath so hushed it hardly comes or goes.
What does it say to hold you in that pose,
that my lips cannot move, my hands invent?
Your words, they never tell me what is meant;
my hands can't touch the peace your body knows.

Pale bloom that gathers light from dusk, your hand
as white as whittled hazel without shine,
the sill and window where you hold quite still.
A word could break the spell... I ache to stand
in for your eyes and grasp this rose in mine
as closely as your hand along the sill.

PETER DALE

Roses, Chrysanthemums

It's late in the day, in the year,
The frost holding off, just.
In the garden you pick dry stalks, hardly looking.
Time to come in,
Time to pick flowers, only now,
And carry them in, summer and autumn bunched,
Toward winter, even the full roses' petals
In no hurry to fall.

It is a slow music we hear
Behind the wind. And the chrysanthemums
Are a slow fire,
A red so dark it glimmers and would go out
But for the yellow that radiates from the core.
Ruffled flutterings here, a harsh odour
As of wood-smoke, and there
Flesh colour, silky, taut in its bland breathing,
Linger and mingle.

Now. Only now.

MICHAEL HAMBURGER

Chrysanthemums, Rowers

The chrysanthemums
which are in the vase on the table
by the window: these

are not the chrysanthemums
which are by the window
on the table
in the vase.

The wind which is annoying you so
and making a mess of your hair, this

is the wind which is messing up your hair;
it is the wind you no longer
want to be annoyed by
when your hair is in a mess.

Only when someone in a photo
stands as large as life
waiting for his death
is he recognized.

They are all standing on the bank,
watching their own birdie;
laughing: all of them.

No one recognizes himself in this photo.
What does suddenly mean in a mirror?
Mirrors never recognize anyone.
What does suddenly mean in a photo?

If soon I see a hand in front
of my face, let me hope
it is a hand of my own

or it is a hand
which wants to belong to me.

If I want to be doing something,
should I have already got up
to want to be doing it;
or should I have wanted

to have it already done:
to get up in such a way
that I should have done it;

and in so doing
the thread being lost,
did as it wanted itself
done, sans rancune:
though nothing had happened,

and I did not wish myself absent,
for I did not know myself like this,
as it was about to happen.

If it brings anything about,
and has forgotten itself,
it is in vain
and for God's sake.

The utter emptiness
in every thing which actually
is, and as such is active,
and merges with the echo
of the last word:

which now refuses to pass
the lips; first caressing

these lips, only to eat away at them
without hesitation: this hopeless lack,
which ties knots all over in water
and is a needle in bread.

Little by little –
they are drawing nearer: 8 rowers,
growing ever further inland

in their mythology:
with each stroke ever further
from home, rowing with all their might;
growing till all the water is gone,
and they fill the whole landscape

to the brim. Eight –
rowing ever further inland;
landscape, for there is
no more water: overgrown
landscape. Landscape,
rowing ever further

inland; land
without rowers; over-
rown land.

HANS FAVEREY
Francis R. Jones

The Summers of Nowhere

Capture the linked hands over a rock
    the shadow eats. Sunfall.
Obsession with camera-angles
    and the diminishing
spill of light behind your blurred profile.

Our forced lips and the night's white blossoms
    echo the lost splash your
bronze arm made – once – water gone, the tide
    swept out and in again,
seasons rubbed on permanent markings.

The dent in the sea, your head's pressure
    under my eye, longing –
the tears on your unchanged expression,
    forever where? An ache
to be naked again in some brown

slanting afternoon. A walk then. Through
    rising avenues of
flowering trees to the ruin in that
    overgrown garden and
the long sea-look over the railings.

My glance near the grain of skin, I brush
    off frequent petals: no
stain – not even light's which greyer days wash
    over. Evening now, our
descent from colour and the need for

warmth shivering over you. My kiss with
    its taste of the moment
ago, the breeze already dying
    which caught every other
word shouted through your laugh from the waves.

HARRY GUEST

Haiku: The Season of Celebrity

With summer comes the
bluebottle; with pleasant fame
comes the journalist.

GAVIN EWART

Last Quarter

Die stillen Kräfte prüfen ihre Breite – RILKE

The moon is eating its heart out
On the downhill stretch of June: last quarter.
And the century is waning fast, making for
The delta, headlong down the slope.

A salvo over the ocean: the fleet is sailing,
South south-west. The sound shatters
Into shrapnel rattling up to the ozone;
A slick lingers three miles long,
A peacock's tail dipped in the sea;
And the hymned sons of the Alps, fearlessly
Crossing the abyss on flimsy bridges,
Have water on the knee: the saving force
May have overlooked the danger growing now,
Feeding on experience, drinking black milk.

By night some goblin garbles the sense
Of a book first loved in the golden
Age of primal balance. Or a glass
On the table shatters, musically. Meanwhile
A few signal-fires go out. There's a fuel
Shortage, they say. So grows a space
Of cross purposes, in silence, like lichen,
While the interpreters write a dictionary,

The language of fear against the language
Of hope, and quarrel about the contents.

But don't let your heart grow heavy
Too fast with expectation: massing forces
Sense only one another and their own
Outline,
            and have started sizing each other up
In your handwriting, darkly, hurriedly.
Count the words you can trust,
Keep the last for yourself.

IVAN V. LALIĆ
Francis R. Jones

The Planes

The heat quivers as the shadows pass,
The heat quivers... but the planes are gone.

Out of the wood the silent deer may stare,
Smell the quick sun and sink into the dark,

Immovable pilots glide on nylon tyres,
The hill's cleavage roll its green pearls.

Out of the field's rank collusion-bloom.
Rank grass suffocates with dew.

Out of each eye more silent than the night
Silent forests regulate the sky.

Delicately sullen – impalpable as God
Valleys float darkening into pines.

Out of the trees buzzards pause – and sleep,
Red Admirals stay on their blue flowers,

But the heat quivers as the shadows pass –
The heat quivers… but the planes are gone.

DONALD WARD

The Desert of Love

A bridge, and a hot concrete road –
the day is emptying its pockets,
laying out, one by one, all its possessions.
You are quite alone in the catatonic twilight.

A landscape like the bed of a wrinkled pit,
with glowing scars, a darkness which dazzles.
Dusk thickens. I stand numb with brightness
blinded by the sun. This summer will not leave me.

Summer. And the flashing heat.
The chickens stand, like burning cherubs,
in the boarded-up, splintered cages.
I know their wings do not even tremble.

Do you still remember? First there was the wind.
And then the earth. Then the cage.
Flames, dung. And now and again
a few wing-flutters, a few empty reflexes.

And thirst. I asked for water.
Even today I hear that feverish gulping,
and helplessly, like a stone, bear
and quench the mirages.

Years are passing. And years. And hope
is like a tin-cup toppled into the straw.

JÁNOS PILINSZKY
János Csokits and Ted Hughes

The Pont Mirabeau

Under the Pont Mirabeau the Seine
  Flows with our loves
 Must I recall again?
Joy always used to follow after pain

   Let the night come: strike the hour
   The days go past while I stand here

Hands holding hands let us stay face to face
  While under this
 Bridge our arms make slow race
Long looks in a tired wave at a wave's pace

   Let the night come: strike the hour
   The days go past while I stand here

Love runs away like running water flows
  Love flows away
 But oh how slow life goes
How violent hope is nobody knows

   Let the night come: strike the hour
   The days go past while I stand here

The days pass and the weeks pass but in vain
  Neither time past

Nor love comes back again
Under the Pont Mirabeau flows the Seine

Let the night come: strike the hour
The days go past but I stay here

GUILLAUME APOLLINAIRE
Oliver Bernard

Part of a Bird

Even now my breast bone's aching
when I remember how I was running
because the smell of petunias invaded everything.
Ah, God, how warm it was around
my legs, bare, long and free
and evening fell over the sea,
over a crowd, gathered there, and over
the strange deserted pavilion
where we played and I
didn't even think about my ugly head
and other children hadn't noticed it either
because we were all running too fast instead
so the transparent eagle of evening wouldn't get us
and the hum of adults from the street
and the sea, the sea, which threatened (protected?)
that *fine del primo tempo*.

It was forever summer, a light summer
a summer of water and sandals, immune
to that alcohol, soon to be called Love,
– and in the deserted pavilion (in vain you'd look for it,
it's either been removed with two fingers
from its ring of earth by War, or by some
useful work, or else forgotten)
we were playing childhood, but, in fact,

I can't remember anyone, I don't think
there was another child apart from me,
because, see, I can only remember
a lonely flight into mystery
staged by the gestures of the sea, I remember
only the happiness, oh God, of leaning
with bare arms and legs on warm stones,
of sloping ground, with grass,
of the innocent air of evening.

Flowers smelled dizzily in that place
where, a little above men and women,
who definitely smelled of tobacco,
hot barbecue and beer, I
was running, unaware of my ugly head,
breaking, in fact, the soft head from the flower
and kissing it on the lips
while the sea also smelled more strongly
than now, it was wilder, its seaweed
darker, and cursed the rocks
even more in the way it whipped them.
It wasn't far from home
to that place, I could run there
and back and no one would miss me,
in four steps and eight jumps I was there,
but, first, I stole from fences
feathers of peacocks left between slats,
most beautiful feathers I've not seen since
with the immense blue green eye
and with golden eyelashes so long
that I was holding a whole bird in my hands
not part of one
and I was tearing at feathers
stuck between slats
tearing at something from the mystery
of those fiendish courtyards
and then I was running toward that deserted pavilion
from the edge of the sea

and I was running round it and through it
through derelict rooms
where mad martins battered themselves against walls,
with the ceiling bursting outside and in, as if within me.

I wore a short sleeveless dress
the color of sand when sun runs out of strength
and in the autumn I should have gone to school,
and the performance of the sea kept breaking my rib cage
to make me more roomy, that's why
my heart was beating and even now the cage in my chest hurts
at the memory of that beat of the sea
while attempting to enter me
especially at evening when flowers fade
without losing their color completely,
staying pink with tea, violet with milk,
losing only their stems in the darkness,
floating, beheaded, at a certain height
above the grass which has also vanished.
This is a tremendous memory,
absolutely unforgettable,
the feeling of a light, unchained body,
invulnerable, perfect, my head
just a natural extension of it,
supervising only its speed and orientation.
Yet I never hurt myself,
I can't remember ever having fallen that summer.
I was light, extremely healthy,
inspired, and if I wasn't flying
it was only because I preferred to run on earth
and not for any other reason.

And after that...
What was I saying? Ah, yes, I had long bare legs
and bare slender arms
and in the deserted pavilion there was this strange coolness
as if an invisible sea had breezed through it...

And after that…
– Where was I? Ah, yes, the flowers full of night…
like sacred smoke
and my lonely flight
through gentle and benevolent mysteries…

And after that?

NINA CASSIAN
Brenda Walker and Andrea Deletant

Flüntern

Summer evening, warm, dull.
Exhausted brambles loll
by a worn wall.

Each crumbling cross,
every tall tombstone, is
camouflaged in moss.

Day's grassy smell
is fresh still:
dusk begins to chill.

Ticks over the red hill
are really swallows: all
muscle, muscle, till

fall of fog. I turn
freely and discern
petals that burn.

Last light on trays of sugar.
I find a poppy, flung here
by some distraught visitor.

Sycamores shrug. Cool silence.
I hope without sense
to breathe dead fragrance.

The odour died when it was born.
This rusty graveyard gate
says what I cannot: *forlorn*.
A weird moan. I am too late.

ALAN MOORE

Fingers Pick Up Sunshine

The sun ties up those figures across the square
in shoelaces   thick bunches of *spago*
        over the span of bleared sight
        transparent fieldscapes lighten
sunbeams loop the edges of roads
        unwinding into Rome
            marble defies sunlight
and dismisses passers-by
the streets we traversed lace up the day
        tramlines meet underneath
            Flies hang above my drink
We tried swinging and dancing
        on crazy crossing lines
            we discovered unloosed
I saw my finger-nails were filled with lemon-peel
                        harsh slivers
        disconnect the urban plan of sunshine
            zebra crossings swirled-out by heat
            I'll pay if you let me
                unpyramid these coins
Let me pass my fingers through the flashing fountain.

LAVINIA MANSEL

Swimming at Midnight

[Near my grandparents' home at the outskirts of town, a stone quarry
was established, then abandoned, nearly a hundred and fifty years
ago. The early blasting hit water, and after many soundings were
taken, the management concluded that they had uncovered a bottom-
less lake, fed, they surmised, by a sizeable underground river.]

Under a pine and confusion:
ah! Tangles of clothes: (come
on, silly, nobody's here:) and
naked as fish, a boy and a girl.
(Nobody comes here: nobody looks:
nobody watches us watching us
watch.) Except the police.
Thighs slide into the moon.
Humbly, into the stars: Mirrored,
flashes a father's red eye, a
blue-bitten mother's red lip: No
Swimming Allowed In The Quarry
At Night. (Anyway, nevertheless
and moreover: feel how warm!) here,
among the reflections. (Feel the
water's mouth and its hands, feel
them imitate mine: can there truly
be any danger?) danger allowed in
the quarry at night? can people
really have drowned? (Now my body
is only water alive, and aeons
ago you were a fish growing
legs –) well, dust to dust, a
curious notion. But quarry water on
dust green with seed! Quarry water
forbidden on land after dark! What
young forms of vegetation emerge.
What new colors of light.

JOHN MATTHIAS

Solar Creation

The sun, of whose terrain we creatures are,
Is the director of all human love,
Unit of time, and circle round the earth

And we are the commotion born of love
And slanted rays of that illustrious star
Peregrine of the crowded fields of birth,

The crowded lanes, the market and the tower
Like sight in pictures, real at remove,
Such is our motion on dimensional earth.

Down by the river, where the ragged are,
Continuous the cries and noise of birth,
While to the muddy edge dark fishes move

And over all, like death, or sloping hill,
Is nature, which is larger and more still.

CHARLES MADGE

'In the oasis of the day'
from LOVE POEMS OF THE VITH DALAI LAMA

In the oasis of the day
        she is with me
but I cannot,
        for reasons of circumspection,
touch her small hand
        too often
or let my eyes
        too lovingly rest
on her amber skin.

When night returns
    and sleep is a mirage
hands
    fresh from her touch
flutter before my eyes,
    eyes
in which hers are reflected
    ogle
me from the darkness.

PETER WHIGHAM

The August Sleepwalker

the stone bell tolls on the seabed
its tolling stirs up the waves

it is august that tolls
there is no sun at high noon in august

a triangular sail swollen with milk
soars over a drifting corpse

it is august that soars
august apples tumble down the ridge

the lighthouse that died long ago
shines in the seamen's gaze

it is august that shines
the august fair comes close on first frost

the stone bell tolls on the seabed
its tolling stirs up the waves

the august sleepwalker
has seen the sun in the night

BEI DAO
Bonnie S. McDougall

Nudes

Slow is the heart
To love what the eye cannot see.
The watcher notes the eternal light
Within the watched, the mortal being.
Great longing the only experience
Experienced under the warm white light:
The nude strolling, taut backs
Of the spirit knees
And stocky beginnings of calves.

Wonder of how things fit
Or are soft enough to permit us in there.
Nests of removable arms
Along the limbs, between bells.
Amphorae, shells, anemones.
Coverts and enclosures
Looking inward on themselves.
Their privacy is thus their protection.
The grapes seem swollen with light.

ANTHONY HOWELL

A Day

Lock up your secrets with a drawer
leave notes in the margin of a favourite book

put a letter in the pillarbox and stand in silence a while
size up passers-by in the wind without misgivings
study shop windows with flashing neon lights
insert a coin in the telephone room
cadge a smoke from the fisherman under the bridge
as the river steamer sounds its vast siren
stare at yourself through clouds of smoke
in the full-length dim mirror at the theatre entrance
and when the curtain has shut out the clamour of the sea of stars
leaf through faded photos and old letters in the lamplight

BEI DAO
Bonnie S. McDougall

The Grammar of Light

Even barely enough light to find a mouth,
and bless both with a meaningless O, teaches,
spells out. The way a curtain opened at night
lets in neon, or moon, or a car's hasty glance,
and paints for a moment someone you love, pierces.

And so many mornings to learn; some
when the day is wrung from damp, grey skies
and rooms come on for breakfast
in the town you are leaving early. The way
a wasteground weeps glass tears at the end of a street.

Some fluent, showing you how the trees
in the square think in birds, telepathise. The way
the waiter balances light in his hands, the coins
in his pocket silver, and a young bell shines
in its white tower ready to tell.

Even a saucer of rain in a garden at evening
speaks to the eye. Like the little fires

from allotments, undressing in veils of mauve smoke
as you walk home under the muted lamps,
perplexed. The way the shy stars go stuttering on.

And at midnight, a candle next to the wine
slurs its soft wax, flatters. Shadows
circle the table. The way all faces blur
to dreams of themselves held in the eyes.
The flare of another match. The way everything dies.

CAROL ANN DUFFY

Summer's End

Lock up this summer in a casket of hay
In a tower of sand in the wind's embrace
In a poppy's chalice lock it lightly
Lock it that it may reappear
Sometime you're alone sometime in winter
Reappear like a scent like a name forgotten
Like a healing sign.

ANNE PENNINGTON

'Frost / lacing'
from LOVE POEMS OF THE VITH DALAI LAMA

Frost
    lacing
late summer
    grass
gives warning
    of autumn
winds.

The honeyed
season
  is over.
The bee
  takes leave
of the flower.
  I
bow myself
  from your bed.

PETER WHIGHAM

Autumn Emotion

Autumn is here, cover my heart somehow –
with a tree-shadow, better still with your shadow.

I am afraid sometimes I shall no longer see you,
I shall grow wings sharp-pointed towards the clouds,
you will hide in a stranger's eye,
he shroud himself in a wormwood leaf.

Then I come closer to stones and am silent,
I take my words and drown them in the sea.
I whistle the moon, and make it rise
into an enormous love.

NICHITA STĂNESCU
Peter Jay and Petru Popescu

Cigolando

Flame torments the sap
where the axe has cut
whimpering in the heat
as it splutters, as it frets
     it goes, it cries
          cigolando, cigolando –
green wood, green wood
talking to itself,
grumbling in the fire.

In the words of Tuscany
fresh wood as it burns,
as it crackles, as it spits,
as it smoulders, it complains
          cigolando, cigolando –
green wood, green wood
talking to itself,
grumbling in the fire.

GAEL TURNBULL

Corona

Autumn eats its leaf out of my hand: we are friends.
From the nuts we shell time and we teach it to walk:
then time returns to the shell.

In the mirror it's Sunday,
in dream there is room for sleeping,
our mouths speak the truth.

My eye moves down to the sex of my loved one:
we look at each other,
we exchange dark words,

we love each other like poppy and recollection,
we sleep like wine in the conches,
like the sea in the moon's blood ray.

We stand by the window embracing, and people look up from
    the street:
it is time they knew!
It is time the stone made an effort to flower,
time unrest had a beating heart.
It is time it were time.

It is time.

PAUL CELAN
Michael Hamburger

Autumn Rain Lament

Looming rain and reckless wind, an indiscriminate
ruins of autumn. The four seas and eight horizons all

gathered into one cloud – you can't tell an ox coming
from horse going, or the muddy Ching from clear Wei.

Wheat-ears are sprouting on the stalk, and millet-
clusters turn black. Nothing arrives from farmers,

not even news. Here in the city, quilts bring
one handful of rice. No one mentions old bargains.

TU FU
David Hinton

Teasing Tu Fu

Here on the summit of Fan-k'o Mountain, it's Tu Fu
under a midday sun sporting his huge farmer's hat.

How is it you've gotten so thin since we parted?
Must be all those poems you've been suffering over.

LI PO
David Hinton

November Elysium

Convalescence. You hang back, at the verge
of the garden. Your background
a peaceful yellow wall's monastery silence.
A tame little wind starts out across the grass. And now,
as if hands assuaged them with holy oils,
your five open wounds, your five senses
feel their healing and are eased.

You are timid. And exultant. Yes,
with your childishly translucent limbs,
in the shawl and coat grown tall,
you are like Alyosha Karamazov.

And like those gentle ones, over yonder,
who are like the child, yes, you are like them.
And as happy too, because
you do not want anything any more.
Only to gleam like the November sun,
and exhale fragrance, lightly as a fir-cone.
Only to bask, like the blest.

JÁNOS PILINSZKY   *Szigliget. November 1958*
János Csokits and Ted Hughes

80

November

The sun has burned the toast of the morning
yet again. Outside our window, late mist
is blown upriver. A thrush begins to sing;
it spits through the flaky Saturday haze.

In the yard there isn't much left of autumn.
Frayed Virginia leaves in the corner
are the summer's disquieting shrapnel –
one year on, an Arts Council grant winds down.

Life that is fragmentary and difficult
has had space to run with outstretched arms;
the blame and lack of love you might have felt
is deeper now. Our child bawls like an alarm

as he has done every night for two years.
Has he found me wanting? I would not wish him
the father I had; hopeless father
who couldn't shield us from the bitching parish

of his own misery. The house was claustrophobic
but only with his own troubles.
It takes so long for a father to learn love,
to ditch the hero for the outstretched hand.

We survive self-knowledge like the memory
of war or a car crash. Not only ourselves
are victims but those who teach us to love.
Each year vanities fall away like leaves

to expose more of our basic structure,
all lopped branches and cankered scars.
Here is memory, here is the recent humus
of trouble. The new gutter sheds tears.

Each gust of wind traps more retreating leaves,
keeps them cornered, makes a damp imprint
of whatever wound. The full year grieves
like a bomb-victim in a basement

and poems come like ballads of the IRA,
under pressure but not admitting love;
primed to defend the hot selected areas.
There, time stands still, more naked and unkind

as years pass overhead. In the shopping mall
of parenthood we are lost. There are fractious walks
in the park, tired shoulders in a wood
or seaside strolls where once was horny talk

before love-making. These, the recurring images
of you, seashells, stones on a sunlit beach,
dolphins, these come to me at the edge
of autumn. They are out of reach

too often now. Pressure of the domestic,
ritual duties of the house. We yearn for more:
domesticity is only interim music.
Love feeds at the edge beyond the seashore

from where it springs. Leaves brush against
the breakfast window. You are asleep once more
after a night of lustful happiness
stolen from the kids. Let's get a divorce

from them and hide in the foliage. Toast
is burning for you through the breakfast news.
The purple dregs of wine in a glass –
Californian, and ripe as figs

against a November wall – have not lost
their sexual taste. The night was seed-filled

and hot as any night in adolescence.
The deep tannin of love still holds.

Only poetry itself is ever autumnal,
wanting to drag in and to store too much.
Better to lose as much again, overturn creels
of possible images. One cannot store touch

or the sensuous moment. The year hangs
now from the cliff of autumn. Winter fills
us already with its compositions, its strange
cleansing light. Rain has washed window-sills

and left them gasping. The haze has lifted.
I breakfast on the good words between
us now. Winter arrives with its gifted
techniques. Leaf fragments adhere to glass, seem

like marmalade pieces left on a plate
or sweet-papers blown across a beach.
I move to the grill to turn up the heat
for more toast. Sunlight is within reach

if only I could touch the lintel of November.
Familiar smells, the grill-pan warms.
November, your birthday. Love breathes upon fear
the way a kiss moistens an exposed arm.

THOMAS McCARTHY

At Midnight

At midnight, far from gladly at that hour,
A small, small boy along the churchyard I
Walked to my father's vicarage; star on star,
Oh how they shone, too richly lit the sky;
    At midnight.

When later I, moved farther though not far,
Must see the loved one, must because she drew me,
Above me stars and northern lights at war,
Going and coming I felt bliss flow through me;
    At midnight.

Until at last the full moon made a rift
So bright, so clear within the dark of me,
And even thought, grown willing, limber, swift
Embraced both past and future easily;
    At midnight.

JOHANN WOLFGANG VON GOETHE   *1818*
Michael Hamburger

Jade-Staircase Grievance

Night long on the jade staircase, white
dew appears, soaks through gauze stockings.

She lets down crystalline blinds, gazes out
through jewel lacework at the autumn moon.

LI PO
David Hinton

'In stone settlements'

In stone settlements when the moon is stone
and gardens have died back to the bare bone
the stars consume to frost, they have their wish,
they wither and flourish.

A wrinkled ocean washes out star-frost,
nothing survives in it, nothing is lost,
far deeper than the cold shadows of fish
I wither and flourish.

As the wild rose in winter is not seen,
the weak scent and the prickle and the green,
but hedges live, the sun is dragonish,
we wither and flourish.

PETER LEVI

Song at Year's End

The year ends thus: northern winds, white snow
shrouding Tung-t'ing Lake and all Hsiao and Hsiang.

Under cold skies, as fishermen tend frozen nets, Mo-yao
tribesmen shoot geese. Their mulberry bows go *twang*.

But Ch'u people like fish, not birds. Let the geese
keep flying south – killing them here is pointless.

Rice was expensive last year. Soldiers starved.
This year, falling prices have ravaged our farmers.

And as officials ride high, stuffed with wine and meat,
the looms in these fleeced straw huts stand empty.

I hear even children are sold now, that it's common
everywhere: love hacked and smothered to pay taxes.

Once, they jailed people for minting coins. But now,
cutting green copper with iron and lead is approved.

Engraved mud would be easier. Good and bad are surely
not the same, but they've long been blended together.

From the walls of ten-thousand kingdoms, painted
horns moan: such sad anthems, will they never stop?

TU FU
David Hinton

The Return

I can never come to terms
with some of my poems
years pass
I can't come to terms with them
yet I cannot disown them
they are bad but they're mine
I gave them birth
they live away from me
indifferent and dead
but there will come a moment when they all
will rush back to me
the successful and the failures
the crippled and the perfect
the ridiculed and the rejected

they will roll into one

TADEUSZ RÓŻEWICZ
Adam Czerniawski

Squall

I have not used my darkness well
nor the Baroque arm that hangs from my shoulder,
nor the Baroque arm of my chair.
The rain moves out in a dark schedule.
Let the wind marry. I know the creation
continues through love. The rain's a wife.
I cannot sleep or lie awake. Looking
at the dead I turn back, fling
my hat into their grandstands for relief.
How goes a life? Something like the ocean
building dead coral.

STANLEY MOSS

Mean Time

The clocks slid back an hour
and stole light from my life
as I walked through the wrong part of town,
mourning our love.

And, of course, unmendable rain
fell to the bleak streets
where I felt my heart gnaw
at all our mistakes.

If the darkening sky could lift
more than one hour from this day
there are words I would never have said
nor have heard you say.

But we will be dead, as we know,
beyond all light.
These are the shortened days
and the endless nights.

CAROL ANN DUFFY

And Suddenly It's Evening

Each of us is alone on the heart of the earth
pierced by a ray of sun:
and suddenly it's evening.

SALVATORE QUASIMODO
Jack Bevan

'How we pass time'

How we pass time, and how it used to pass:
a poem as anonymous as the grass.

What sleep, what a parody of perfect
sprinkled the infancy of God's elect;

and how time altered when I was a boy,
the single blue colour of liberty
ran loosely for ever around the sky;

what young eyes, what wisdom, it was a fruit
that stood still in the wisdom of God,
the apple is sour, the apple is sweet.

How we pass time, and how it used to pass:
as fresh and endless and common as grass.

The clock will keep time now in the bad times
chiming live among the echoes of chimes;

how old time has become, how life has been
music played over again and again,
and the foam whiter than the sea was green;

I am hungry for that air and the wild cries,
to taste how everlasting the sea is,
green dark of love, the harsh light blue of skies.

How we pass time, and how it used to pass,
an infinite and perfect world of grass.

PETER LEVI

You Lie Down to Sleep

You lie down to sleep
with no one to kiss you goodnight
and within moments to abandon you there.

You lie on your side, one leg flung
across the entire width of the bed,
in the certainty that sleep is near.

You savour this certainty
like sweet, fresh water,
like being received in your saviour's arms.

DANIEL WEISSBORT

'Sleep wrapped you in green leaves'

from MYTHISTOREMA

Quid πλατανὼν opacissimus?

Sleep wrapped you in green leaves like a tree
you breathed like a tree in the quiet light
in the limpid spring I looked at your face:
eyelids closed, eyelashes brushing the water.
In the soft grass my fingers found your fingers
I held your pulse a moment
and felt elsewhere your heart's pain.

Under the plane tree, near the water, among laurel
sleep moved you and scattered you
around me, near me, without my being able to touch the whole
   of you –
one as you were with your silence;
seeing your shadow grow and diminish,
lose itself in the other shadows, in the other
world that let you go yet held you back.

The life that they gave us to live, we lived.
Pity those who wait with such patience
lost in the black laurel under the heavy plane trees
and those, alone, who speak to cisterns and wells
and drown in the voice's circles.
Pity the companion who shared our privation and our sweat
and plunged into the sun like a crow beyond the ruins,
without hope of enjoying our reward.

Give us, outside sleep, serenity.

GEORGE SEFERIS
Edmund Keeley and Philip Sherrard

Blue Dreamlight Shaman Song

In the blue dreamlight, the blue dreamlight,
      in the blue dreamlight,
         the blue.
An old man is afraid, a hunter is afraid,
      in the blue dreamlight,
         the blue.
A young woman, a young wise woman,
      in the blue dreamlight,
      in the blue.
In the blue dreamlight, blue,
      speak, crouched by water,
      in the blue dreamlight,
         the blue.
We have brown and snowy circles,
      in the blue dreamlight,
         the blue,
we have long circles under the mountains,
      in the blue.
Great mountain drinks from sky-hand,
      the blue dreamlight,
         the blue.
Great mountain drinks:
grass, rock, moss, satisfy their thirst,
      in the blue dreamlight,
      in the blue.
We have chains of little families,
      in the blue dreamlight,
we have chains of sojourners and women
      in the blue dreamlight,
        in the blue dreamlight,
            in the blue.
From beginning to the end,
      blue dreamlight in the blue,
from beginning to the middle,
      blue dreamlight in the blue.

Whale, raven, bear, salmon, fox,
     in the blue dreamlight,
      in the blue.
Whale, man, gull, dog, ptarmigan,
     in the blue dreamlight,
      in the blue.
O it is now,
     and it was then,
O it is now,
     and it was then,
  in the blue dreamlight,
     in the blue dreamlight,
      the blue.

TOM LOWENSTEIN

Sleep, Silhouette

Sleep, silhouette, beneath night's bridge
in a gown of water. My voice I give,
weak with insistence, to the sharp air;
the key is taken by those xylophone lights
that dint the black ebb we are lapped in.
Still world. What do I ask for? Names
for what we are, our deeps perform.
Cold shadow, sleep now, one day's love
having drained us with sweet tribulation.
We know of pangs, for bodies feel
but only the mind remembers. Slide
into this numb death of satiety,
a forced integument of clammy rest,
green lips apart, I with no name
to designate our effort and our loss.

A tide, but not of sleep, steals you.
Behind the dear brown of your eye's gristle

I hear the enchantment of bruised sobs.
I know the pain. Rehearse me while I live.
Recall, moist bulletin, my tongue.
And my ambassador fingers grown aware
liquidity means use, meant readiness.
I was not marginal; dealt close –
scorning your prelude whimper – stung
your red interior with singing pains,
longer joys scattering then, until
from crotch to chin our sweaty bodies held
and we arrived, gyrating breast to breast,
at motion like the motion of a stone
wherein we learned duration, beyond grief.

We were not satisfied. Who is, alive?
The human fascinated. We forsook
the mood of granite; eddied to brinks,
testing disintegration till we fell,
being weary of stone, for only flesh keeps time.
Rested. Resumed. And the day died.
A cold wind came and still no name
for the scared sorrows lapping our arched bones.
No name. An eye – no name – behind the moon
explores me with your stare, that's all.

Until I know. Your arms: in them
I have shown mercy to the egregious moon,
to the pathetic stars and to my flesh.
Now like a boom a recognition breathes.
I've found content more final than a name.
Upon your lids darkens the bruise of sorrow.
Sleep hardens our insoluble lives.
Lights die. But the world's over now.

ALAN MARSHFIELD

Sin: A Dream

I was so busy confessing –
'His noble confession', you called it –
that we lost her.
At the exit to the store
I distracted you...
And then she was lost in the crowd.

I implored God,
so fraught that I woke myself up,
sweating, cursing, and lamenting
and at the same time assuring myself:
You've learnt a lesson
and there's no harm done
because it was just a dream.

And yet
for certain sins, though you wake,
there is no forgiveness either.

DANIEL WEISSBORT

A Translator's Nightmare

I think it must have been in Limbo where,
As Dante says, the better poets share
Old friendships, rivalries, once famous fights
And, now they've left it, set the world to rights.
As I was being hustled through in transit
To God knows what damned hole, I thought I'd chance it
And chat to some of the assembled great ones
Who looked as bored as trapped theatre patrons
Who've paid good cash and find they hate the show...
I picked on one: 'I rather doubt you know...'
He started up and peered at me: 'Know you,

You snivelling fool? Know you? Of course I do!
You ruined my best poem. Look who's here...'
He turned to his companions with a sneer,
'Traducer and destroyer of our art,
The biggest stink since Beelzebub's last fart.'
They jostled round, each shouting out his curses,
'You buried me with your insipid verses...'
'You left out my best metaphor, you moron...'
'You missed my meaning or they set no store on
An accurate rendition where you come from.'
'He comes from where they send the deaf and dumb from,
He got my metre wrong...', ' He missed my rhymes',
'He missed puns I don't know how many times,
Then shoved his own in...' But I turned and fled,
Afraid that in a moment I'd be dead
A second time, torn limb from spectral limb.

A mist came down and I was lost. A dim
Shape beckoned; thinking it must be my guide,
I ran for reassurance to his side.
But it was someone I'd not seen before,
An old man bent beside the crumbling shore
Of Lethe's stream. He stared a long time, then
'Did you translate?'. I screamed, 'Oh not again!'
But as I backed off one quick claw reached out;
He clutched my coat and with a piercing shout
(He didn't look as though he had it in him)
Cried, 'We've a guest! Who'll be the first to skin him?'
Then added, 'Just my joke now; stay awhile,
The crowd in these parts is quite versatile,
Though we've one thing in common, all of us:
When you were curious, and courteous,
Enough to translate poems from our tongue
All of us gathered here were not among
The chosen ones.' I looked around – a crowd
Now hemmed us in and from it soon a loud
Discordant murmur rose: 'Please, why not mine?'
'You did Z's poems, my stuff's just as fine...'

'The greatest critics have admired my verse…'
'You worked on crap that's infinitely worse
Than my worst lines.' '*Some* of my stuff's quite good –
You will allow that? – It's not *all* dead wood?
Why then…?' and slowly the reproaches turned
To begging, bragging, angry tears that burned
Their way into my sorry soul.

                                    Once more
I ran and saw my guide, tall on the shore
– The other shore – of Lethe. 'Rescue me!'
I called, 'Get me to where I have to be
For all eternity…' He smiled: 'My dear,
You've reached your special hell, it's here. It's here.'

DICK DAVIS

First Fear

Every corner or alley, every moment's good
for the killer who's been stalking me
night and day for years.
Shoot me, shoot me – I tell him
offering myself to his aim
in the front, the side, the back –
let's get it over with, do me in.
And saying it I realize
I'm talking to myself alone.
                                    But
it's no use, it's no use. On my own
I cannot bring myself to justice.

VITTORIO SERENI
Marcus Perryman and Peter Robinson

Keeping Steady

Water-borne I watch the boat's shadow
flow over lichen-covered rock,
shadow on shadow as if the lichen
too were on its slow way past.
Air-borne I watch mottled islands
drift with the ease of clouds. I've left
days of my life on one of them and now
I carry the island, an invisible weight.

On land again, still seeing the curved
earth I lean to stay upright
then settle my newest memories
on an old point of balance. It's like the pause
clock-hands make at midnight.

ROBIN FULTON

3 a.m.

I'll give him a minute longer
before I break the news.
Another minute of innocence and rest.
He is in the thicket of dreams
he will still be struggling with
as he stirs himself to take my call
wondering who in Christ's name
this could be.
           One more minute, then,
to let him sleep through what
he's just about to wake to.

DENNIS O'DRISCOLL

Perhaps the Heart

The sharp smell of the limes will drown
in the night of rain. The time
of joy, the frenzy, with its shattering lightning bite
will be vain.
Numbness is all that remains,
a remembered gesture, a syllable,
but like a slow flight of birds
in a haze of mist. And still you wait
for I know not what, my lost one; perhaps
a decisive hour that evokes
the beginning or end: the same fate
from now on. Here the black smoke of the fires
still parches the throat. If you can,
forget that taste of sulphur,
and the fear. Words weary us,
rising again from a flailed water;
perhaps the heart is left us, perhaps the heart.

SALVATORE QUASIMODO
Jack Bevan

Giacomo Leopardi in Naples

Do you know that something very strange is happening
to me?... When I think of my impending destruction,
I seem to see myself lying in a ditch, with a crowd
of ribald fools dancing on my belly.
     —LEOPARDI TO PAOLINA RANIERI, 1837

Shall we, my sweet tooth, consume another ice?
I signal Vito *il padrone* whose grave nod bespeaks the substance
Of any man who knows what his art is,
And the making of ices is surely one.
I must beware my friend Ranieri who would deny me this sad
     pleasure

Although my clock almost strikes twelve.
Antonio Ranieri, who, if I could believe in God, would drive
    Him from my table
And then sermonize on the evils of chocolate –
This man whom I love plugs my brain with his cackle:
'The mood on the Largo della Carità spells plague,
And still, my Giacomo, you cannot bear to leave Naples.
What will you not gamble for Vito's matchless ices?'

All Naples is one huge, sleepless pantomime
As was that other place the gods covered with ashes.
The mountain broods beneath its canopy of smoke
While these revellers with their booming voices and pointed
    shoes,
These plumed creatures whom progress loves,
Make corridors in air.
The pursuit of happiness brings them none.
They drape the skeleton of all things with their festering
    pride,
And fearing the tumble through endless space wage war upon
    silence.
Should they win, where then my verses?

The ancients scorned the man who sups alone,
And yet what deeper shame than to be seen from above
    slobbering over an ice?
Or to be judged by the stains on one's clothes?
I should banish all pleasure to the cubicle.
Who, if suddenly the world broke, would probe the rubble,
And finding here my skull with a spoon stuck inside,
Summon up the pale flesh which covered the bone?
Would they conclude this man of words loved so much the life
    he could not have
That he loved death even more?
They shall review my bones from all sides,
Saying the darkness which goes so deep can only be pure
    sunlight in reverse,

Or, as that bastard Florentine said of me,
'There is no God because I am a hunchback;
I am a hunchback because there is no God.'
Bah, I'd rather that Vito bury me.
The place is suddenly hopping alive,
As if from nowhere all these people pressing close, their breath
stale
And their talk even worse.
I shall command my own table.

I was born in a sepulchre.
When I consider the years swaddled in that dark place,
A cold, high room where the aching for knowledge doubled me,
Small wonder the world's light blinded me.
And now I shall perish where the mountain hugging the shore
Makes a cradle.

I must praise the bread a certain woman bakes.
You will not find such bread anywhere outside Naples although
Genoa comes close,
And this madonna of the loaves is Genovese.
The world becomes for me a narrow place,
A simple truth Ranieri might consider when he comes to write
my notice,
Although I fear the enthusiasm which in him outweighs
intelligence
One day may become menace.
Already I gauge my own death in his voice,
And when he asks what my needs are, I say only those which he
would deny me.
A doctor stands always by his side.
'You must quit Naples,' they tell me, 'Go, before the cholera
comes.'
I shall not forsake the bread this woman bakes.
The fewer my needs, the more precise they must be
Should they make the narrow world bearable.

Perhaps I should love Paolina more.
The sister of Antonio Ranieri reads me verses,
And although Ariosto, Tasso, Dante sound strange on a
    southern tongue
I would swap heaven for the bright lamp in her voice.
She is so completely without malice.
The other night she stumbled over some passage;
A deep blush spread through the awkward silence,
And it was as though she wished she could hide behind the
    language,
Thus spare me the illusion of love.
La donna che non si trova.
The women on the Largo della Carità glide,
And if they seem to me of a world other than the one which
    spurned me
The plain girl who reads me verses
Shall be my earthly guide.

Vito,
      Antonio Ranieri,
           Paolina…

I will write in my book of consolations the names
Of those whom destiny might otherwise blur on stone.
The critics and poetasters must fend for themselves.
They would burn up the whole language for a single shred of
    praise,
Yet I alone give them credence.
When finally the swine dance attendance on me
(And yes, that one in particular who mocked my shape)
Will they say this man of words sugared his lemonade so it
    became
A thick syrup galvanizing the flies?
An age whose minds are clogged with obscenities will note
What Vito, a man of honour, commits to silence.

A peasant from the Abruzzi plays on his bagpipe.
Ah, that I should have wasted breath bullying language
When this man with his solemn music pulls darkness over the
    bay of Naples.
Although God hides and Signor Leopardi must die
A sudden gladness swamps me.

Scende la luna; e si scolora il mondo.

Almighty blindness conquers me,
Yet still I see my silver spoon rise
And then dip towards the round horizon of my table where
    God is a flickering candle.
Perhaps Vito, the purveyor of ices, can say more of what
    pleasure is
And what place it has on the curve of the infinite than any
    struggler with rhymes.
On this night, however, let it be said some deep chord ancient
    and spare,
As pure in sound as anything Pindar wrote,
Cut a swathe through the clattering age.

A painted wagon thunders over the cobblestones.
Already I can hear from another, darker vehicle the hooded voice
Crying, '*Chi ha morti, li cavi!*'
But what is death when Madama Girolama bakes
The bread that shall always carry the sound of her name?
Vito places the chairs on the tables;
Moonlight sweeps the floor bare.
This is a strange forest which I must now leave.
Say Giacomo Leopardi found peace at Naples.

MARIUS KOCIEJOWSKI

*A young woman has mixed feelings about the patchwork
quilt she has just completed:*

Strange how two colours that combine
So neatly when compared alone
Can clash, now that the thing is whole.
I thought that I had planned it all:
I looked at books, gave careful thought
To getting every colour right,
Never afraid to change my mind,
Unpicking rows from end to end
At times; giving my very best;
Aiming at something that would last.
But now I feel this red's too hard;
I should have put that green outside;
The more I look, the less I like
The pattern of the central block.
Of course it's not completely wrong.
It's almost like a living thing,
A plant or child, that won't give in,
Entirely, to a perfect plan.
It moves along its own strange track.
Perhaps it's through a kind of luck,
Rather than all this thought and fuss,
That sometimes one achieves success.
All I can do is start again.
I think I know my next design.

WILLIAM RADICE

Coolie

Coolie cane chop.
Coolie go
      go
          only softly-softly
  Rickshaw
  Car
  Dragon-carriage
Coolie pull rickshaw.
Coolie pull car.
Coolie pull dragon-carriage
        only softly-softly
Coolie go foot.
Coolie beard white.
Coolie sleepy.
Coolie hungry.
Coolie old.
Coolie bean poppyseed little child
big wicked man beat little Coolie
        only softly-softly
  Rickshaw
  Car
  Dragon-carriage
Who pull rickshaw?
Who pull car?
Who pull dragon-carriage?
Suppose Coolie dead.
Coolie dead.
Coolie no-o-o-t know dead!
Coolie immortal.
        only softly-softly

SÁNDOR WEÖRES
Edwin Morgan

The Story of a Story

Once upon a time there was a story

It ended
Before its beginning
And it began
After its end

Its heroes entered it
After their death
And left it
Before their birth

Its heroes talked
About some earth about some heaven
They said all sorts of things

The only thing they didn't say
Was what they didn't know
That they are only heroes in a story

In a story that ends
Before its beginning
And that begins
After its end

VASKO POPA
Anne Pennington

The Master

A Zen Narrative

TO HIDEHIKO SHINDO
WHO TAUGHT ME THE BEGINNINGS
OF JAPANESE ARCHERY

I

'What's that?' said Ki-sho,
pointing at a bamboo bow
    hanging on the wall.
    His father told him,
and from that moment Ki-sho
    craved to learn the art.

    Seeking a master,
he heard that one Hi-ei
    could not be excelled.
    (At ninety paces,
Hi-ei never once missed
    marks on willow leaves.)

    Ki-sho went to him,
and Hi-ei took him in
    as a disciple.

II

    The first lesson was
learning how to keep the eyes
    wide without blinking.

    Ki-sho went back home,
crept under his wife's loom, and,
    his face turned upward,
    stared at the pedals
of the warp-control moving
    quickly up and down.
    His wife, not knowing

why he was staring like that,
     was most embarrassed
     and began to laugh,
but Ki-sho, angry, told her
     to keep on weaving.

     All day long, he stared
at the pedals; and, after
     two years, stopped blinking.

     He was so adept
a pin stuck in his eyelid
     could not make him blink.

     If sparks from the fire
or clouds of ashes flew up,
     his eyes never moved.
     He could not in fact
close his eyes: even in sleep
     they stayed wide open.
     Then a spider spun
a web between the lashes
     of one of his eyes.

     Full of confidence,
he told Hi-ei he had
     learned the first lesson.

III

     The master just smiled,
and said Ki-sho had to learn
     the second lesson –
     how to look at things,
how to make the small seem great
     and the faint distinct.

Ki-sho went back home
and took a flea from the hem
    of his undershirt,
    tied it with a hair
from his head, and hung it up
    in the south window.
    For two whole days, he
stared at the writhing insect:
    it was a mere flea;
    but ten days later,
due to his concentration,
    it appeared larger.
    Ninety days later,
there was no doubt in his mind
    it matched a silk-worm.

    The brightness of spring
changed to the heat of summer.
    Wild geese crossed the sky.
    Ki-sho persevered.
Snow fell. The flea was renewed
    time and time again.
    Then, quite suddenly,
three years later, Ki-sho slapped
    his knee and stood up:
    the flea was as big
as a horse! He went outside:
    pigs were high as hills,
    horses were mountains,
and men were higher than clouds!
    Ki-sho danced for joy.

    He looked at the flea,
took a fish-bone for a bow,
    an arrow of thorn,
    and, at the first try,
without severing the hair,
    he pierced the flea's heart.

Hi-ei was pleased,
slapped his chest, and gave him
        praise for the first time.

    IV
    Hi-ei began
to lead Ki-sho into deep
        secrets of the art.

    He was quick to learn.
Helped by the five years' basic
        training of his eyes,
        in a mere ten days
he could shoot marked willow leaves
        at ninety paces.
    Twenty days later –
a sake-cup of water
        on his right elbow –
        he could draw a bow
of strong bamboo and never
        spill a single drop.
    After thirty days,
he had mastered shooting with
        a hundred arrows:
        the first arrow hit
the bull's-eye, the second hit
        the first, and so on,
        arrows end to end –
a perfect line from target
        to bowstring. 'Well done!'
        Hi-ei was pleased,
and told his pupil he had
        nothing more to learn.

    Ki-sho, however,
could not be satisfied till
        he was sole master,
        the best in the world;

and to be that he needed
        to kill Hi-ei.
    He chose a moment,
nocked an arrow, drew the bow,
        aimed at his master;
        but Hi-ei saw,
and answered with an arrow
        quicker than Ki-sho's.
    The shafts met half-way
point to point, hovered, then fell
        gently to the ground.
    Three times this happened,
till the master had none left;
        Ki-sho had one more.
    He took aim, and shot;
but Hi-ei snatched a branch
        of pine and stopped it;
        and Ki-sho, convinced
he could never defeat him,
        stood in amazement.
    Master and pupil
ran to each other, embraced,
        and wept tears of joy.

    Then Hi-ei told
Ki-sho to go to Kan-yo,
        the greatest master.
    'Our art is a game,'
he said, 'compared to Kan-yo's.
        You must learn from him.'

    V

    So Ki-sho went west,
over the pass of Taiko,
        to Kaku mountain.
    There he met Kan-yo,
an aged man with sheep-like eyes
        and a long white beard.

Eager to impress
Kan-yo, Ki-sho drew his bow
    and shot at five geese.
The arrow passed through
all five, and the birds dropped down
    from the clear blue sky.
    Kan-yo gave a smile.
'You have standard skill,' he said,
    'but you seem to know
    nothing of the art
of shooting with no-arrow
    and no-bow, my friend.'

He took the pupil
to the edge of a cliff where
    far below Ki-sho,
    his senses reeling,
could see a winding river,
    a mist of green trees.
    Goat-like Kan-yo leapt
to an overhanging rock
    and beckoned Ki-sho:
    'Come here, and show me
once again the splendid skills
    you say you've acquired.'
    Ki-sho changed places
with Kan-yo, and stood trembling
    on the balanced rock.
    He nocked an arrow,
but just then a pebble went
    rattling down the cliff.
    Ki-sho watched it fade,
then, sweating at the heels, fell
    prostrate on the rock.
    Kan-yo laughed and said:
'Now, my friend, I will show you
    the art of shooting.'
    'But where is your bow?'

The old man's hands were empty.
　　He smiled at Ki-sho:
　　'While you need a bow
and arrow, your shooting is
　　just the art of art.
　　The art of no-art
needs neither bow nor arrow.'
　　He gazed at the sky.
　　High above, a kite
was circling, a minute speck
　　hardly visible.
　　Then Kan-yo fitted
an invisible arrow
　　to an unseen bow,
　　drew the bow-string back
as full as the full moon, and
　　let the arrow fly.

　　The black kite, not one
feather fluttering, with no
　　sound, dropped like a stone.

　　Ki-sho, terrified,
began to catch a glimpse of
　　the depths of the art.

　　VI

　　Nine years he stayed there.
No one knows what disciplines
　　he had to master.

　　When he came back home,
people were surprised to see
　　how much he had changed.
　　His face, once so proud
and confident, was now dull,
　　half-witted, dunce-like.
　　Hi-ei, however,

was not surprised. 'Yours,' he said,
'is a master's face!'

Ki-sho had become
the most renowned of archers,
famous far and wide.
Everybody hoped
he would demonstrate his art,
but he never did.
Indeed, it appeared
he had lost his bow somewhere
and had no arrows.

'True deed is no deed,'
he mumbled, 'and the true art
is never to shoot.'
And everybody knew
he was the greatest archer
that had ever lived.

He went back home, and
sitting down beside his wife
near the south window,
he happened to glance
at his father's bamboo bow
hanging on the wall.

Smiling, he turned to
his wife, pointed at the bow,
and murmured: 'What's that?'

GAVIN BANTOCK

Moving House

Like a life that dies on a summer's afternoon,
The blood in the veins of the house
Is weakening now. Was strong and thick
In the arteries, and livelier still
In the children's songs.
The inquisitive sun is sprinkling light
On the chairs, the tables, the cups and plates,
And the strange black van that is waiting.

There were doors in the house that opened
Only at times, for the keys were lost.
But the other doors swung on their hinges
And the rooms became worn to the shape
Of the lives that fitted them.

There were faces that came out of the mist
Surrounding us, stayed for a time,
Now are dissolved in the cherry tree's flowering,
Or preserved in a dream that recurs.

Now the rooms are all disordered by emptiness,
Sudden exposure of dust, and paint that is peeling.
In the drive an armchair sags in the sunlight,
And holly and yew are sheltering things
Like displaced persons, all huddled and bruised
Waiting their next rough handling.

HEATHER BUCK

In Rooms

In rooms we never enter
Embossed hoopoes cover
A screen of red velvet.

The polished marble fireplace
Mottles its black surface
With crushed specks of bivalve.

Starched antimacassars
Arch over the headrests
Of buffed leather armchairs.

So... how best to continue
Now that we are privy
To the intimate groundplan?

Shall we draw an armchair
Up to the speckled fireplace
Screened by the flocks of velvet?

Already the birds are clouds.
Already the stone is wood.
Already the chair is a stone.

Already in the corners
Of the room we never entered
Dusk is beginning.

DAVID HARTNETT

Men at Forty

Men at forty
Learn to close softly
The doors to rooms they will not be
Coming back to.

At rest on a stair landing,
They feel it moving

Beneath them now like the deck of a ship,
Though the swell is gentle.

And deep in mirrors
They rediscover
The face of the boy as he practices tying
His father's tie there in secret,

And the face of that father,
Still warm with the mystery of lather.
They are more fathers than sons themselves now.
Something is filling them, something

That is like the twilight sound
Of the crickets, immense,
Filling the woods at the foot of the slope
Behind their mortgaged houses.

DONALD JUSTICE

Rent

If you want my apartment, sleep in it
but let's have a clear understanding:
the books are still free agents.

If the rocking chair's arms surround you
they can also let you go,
they can shape the air like a body.

I don't want your rent, I want
a radiance of attention
like the candle's flame when we eat,

I mean a kind of awe
attending the spaces between us –
Not a roof but a field of stars.

JANE COOPER

Leaf-Huts and Snow-Houses

There's not much to
these verses, only
a few words piled up
at random.
I think
nonetheless
it's fine
to make them, then
for a little while
I have something like a house.
I remember leaf-huts
we built
when we were small:
to creep in and sit
listening to the rain,
feel alone in the wilderness,
drops on your nose
and your hair –
Or snow-houses at Christmas,
to creep in and
close the hole with a sack,
light a candle and stay there
on cold evenings.

OLAV H. HAUGE
Robin Fulton

The Little Box

The little box grows her first teeth
And her little length grows
Her little width her little emptiness
And everything she has

The little box grows and grows
And now inside her is the cupboard
She was in before

And she grows and grows and grows
And now inside her is the room
And the house and town and land
And the world she was in before

The little box remembers her childhood
And by wishing really hard
Becomes a little box again

Now inside the little box
Is the whole world all teeny-weeny
Easy to slip in your pocket
Easy to steal easy to lose

Look after the little box

VASKO POPA
Anne Pennington and Francis R. Jones

The House

I remember silences:
the silence of the bedroom
in which someone had gone mad;

the silence of corridors
where nobody went or came
and nothing was ever said;

I remember the silence
of the backyard at noonday
with the cat curled on a stone;

the silence of mezzotints
leapt at or lapped by shadow
when the evening firelight shone;

most of all I remember
the silence of secrecy:
of not knowing what was wrong.

This silence was my mother,
clenched on an ancient sorrow,
her harsh threnody unsung.

TONY CONNOR

I

La casa se construye con lo que ahí encontramos
(con crin ligaban la argamasa – había caballos)
y con lo que traemos (la rima anda escondida):
para su tiempo, espacio – tiempo para su espacio.

Mas nacemos en casas que no hicimos.
(Vuelve la rima, puente entre líneas.)
El sol desenterradas imágenes revuelve
y me devuelve aquella casa en ruinas,

no por mí: por el tiempo deshecha – se revela
en su marcha la rima, la inoída,
frágil contra su espacio – y disonante.

El tiempo la deshace y el tiempo la rehace;
la rima, sol que nace de eco en eco,
la ilumina: ya no es espacio sino tiempo.

OCTAVIO PAZ AND CHARLES TOMLINSON

'Loving the rituals'

Loving the rituals that keep men close,
Nature created means for friends apart:

pen, paper, ink, the alphabet,
signs for the distant and disconsolate heart.

PALLADAS
Tony Harrison

FROM *House*

I

One builds a house of what is there
(horsehair bonded the plaster when horses were)
and of what one brings (the rhyme concealed):
space into its time, time to its space.

Yet we are born in houses we did not make.
(The rhyme returns, a bridge between the lines.)
The sun revolves its buried images
to restore to mind that ruined house once more

time and not I unmade – the rhyme revealed
only by the unheard pace of time,
and fragile yet dissonant against its space.

Time unmakes and builds the house again:
and rhyme, a sun brought, echo by echo, to birth,
illuminates, unspaces it back to time.

CHARLES TOMLINSON AND OCTAVIO PAZ

A Guest

I've had asthma now for years. But here
Beside this river, our *ch'i*-sited
Home is new. Even simple noise scarce,
Its healing joy and ease are uncluttered.

When someone visits our thatch house, I
Call the kids to straighten my farmer's cap,
And from the sparse garden, gather young
Vegetables – a small handful of friendship.

TU FU
David Hinton

From Ashes

Sometimes a man comes home to find his house
burnt to the floor and no fire left to fight.
Stray sparks glint between splinters of glass.
No one is home and no home stands and it is a cold night.

And the scene is deep in trees. And no moon shows.
Trees never caught and they keep him there in the dark.
Pine trees sifting the wind bend and brush elbows,
differing whether he'll bother setting to work

to set to rights the black hulks of his beams
leaning unevenly over his late concerns –
the ashy pulp of papers and books whose names
are hard now to remember. Now he learns

to notice the basic, charred bones of the house,
bent pipes, fused wires, a battered sink –
boring necessities made precious by loss.
Hearing the gossipy pines, he tries to think:

Was it lightning? Did the cat chew on a wire?
Did the wind help? Why didn't he live in town,
where neighbors are near and trees are tame and fire
attracts attention? Nobody's house burns down

nowadays. All his woes are out of style,
like his address. Who else happens to be
deprived of a big red hook-and-ladder while
flames eat up his shingles? He can see

only so far: Privacy didn't pay.
His one pet lies minus her nine lives.
Now what? Walk off and leave it, the way
men will abandon bad cars or their wives?

O ashes will all be cold by morning, morning,
mutter the pines, his proxy family, till he
turns on his heel, hard. But he hears a ping
down by his foot: this is that extra key,

scuffed from under what was a doormat. When
he holds it in his hand his trees become
silent, as if suddenly seared. A man
clings to his title. Sometimes a man comes home.

ROBERT B. SHAW

Poet's Refuge

TO THE MEMORY OF VERONICA PORUMBACU
TOLYA BACONSKY MILO PETROVEANU AND MIHAI GAFIȚA

A few poets old friends
Met for supper
In a house in Bucharest

The earthquake broke into their supper
And crashed the house to the ground

The salvage team is looking for them
In the wreckage of concrete glass
Flesh and rags

A young soldier flings out his arms
White with plaster to the elbows

We won't find them here
They're in their poems

VASKO POPA
Anne Pennington and Francis R. Jones

Places we love exist only through us,
Space destroyed is only illusion in the constancy of time,
Places we love we can never leave,
Places we love together, together, together,

And is this room really a room, or an embrace,
And what is beneath the window: a street or years?
And the window is only the imprint left by
The first rain we understood, returning endlessly,

And this wall does not define the room, but perhaps the night
Your son began to move in your sleeping blood,
A son like a butterfly of flame in your hall of mirrors,
The night you were frightened by your own light,

And this door leads into any afternoon
Which outlives it, forever peopled
With your casual movements, as you stepped,
Like fire into copper, into my only memory;

When you go, space closes over like water behind you,
Do not look back: there is nothing outside you,
Space is only time visible in a different way,
Places we love we can never leave.

IVAN V. LALIĆ
Francis R. Jones

In the Village of My Forefathers

One hugs me
One looks at me with wolf eyes
One takes off his hat
So I can see him better

Each one asks me
Do you know who I am

Unknown old men and women
Usurp the names
Of boys and girls of my memory

And I ask one of them
Tell me old chap
Is George Kurja
Still alive

That's me he answers
In a voice from the other world

I stroke his cheek with my hand
And silently beg him to tell me
Whether I am alive still too

VASKO POPA
Anne Pennington

A Wild Joy

A number of ancient customs are still observed in this part
    of the world but none is more curious than the yearly
    capture of a joy.

That is, a wild one. Some are still natural in the country
    districts. By tradition the whole town participates in the
    pursuit. Crowds come from great distances to watch, as,
    except for circus specimens, they know them only by
    description.

'Poor thing!' I said to one of the spectators, 'to be tracked
    down like that! See how it trembles!'

He corrected me. 'On the contrary, they are remarkably
hardy and can survive for long periods under conditions
of the greatest privation.

'What's more, they are treacherous. It's no secret that more
than one great man has come to grief here, thinking he
might get one for his own.'

GAEL TURNBULL

Hunting

I have never run after words,
All I have sought
Was their long
Silver shadows,
Dragged by the sun through grass
Or drawn by the moon over the sea;
I have never hunted
Anything but the shadows of words –
It is very skilful hunting
Learned from old people
Who know
That within a word
Nothing is more precious
Than its shadow
And they no longer have a shadow,
The words that have sold their souls.

ANA BLANDIANA
Peter Jay and Anca Cristofovici

Quatrain Without Sparrows, Helpful Bells or Hope

FROM THE IRISH

My world has been laid low, and the wind blows
Alexander's ashes and all who killed for us.
Troy is gone. And Ulster's wild sorrow,
It too, like Troy, like the English, it too will pass.

THOMAS McCARTHY

After Any Wreck

Here
we have come at last
to a place out of the wind –
we look down from the doorway
of a small stone hut,
peer through mist and drizzle
for the lost sunlit land

and know
that there the waves are gnawing polished beams,
night is fallen on bright columns,
and the sea-sifted weed
floats tranquil over golden tiles.

In this hard refuge
on a hill above Atlantis,
hear only how
a cry from the despairing sea
is broken on the wind.

SALLY PURCELL

'Three rocks, a few burnt pines'

from MYTHISTOREMA

Bottle in the sea

Three rocks, a few burnt pines, a lone chapel
and farther above
the same landscape repeated starts again:
three rocks in the shape of a gateway, rusted,
a few burnt pines, black and yellow,
and a square hut buried in whitewash;
and still farther above, many times over,
the same landscape recurs level after level
to the horizon, to the twilit sky.

Here we moored the ship to splice the broken oars,
to drink water and to sleep.
The sea that embittered us is deep and unexplored
and unfolds a boundless calm.
Here among the pebbles we found a coin
and threw dice for it.
The youngest won it and disappeared.

We put to sea again with our broken oars.

GEORGE SEFERIS
Edmund Keeley and Philip Sherrard

The Hitch-Hiker's Curse on Being Passed By

(EXCERPTS)

The Curse of Your Wheels to you!
May your inlet manifold get choked
While your head gaskets are leaking
And may your camshaft lobes wear out.
Although your cylinders each crack,
A man will be found to replace them,
Wrecking as he does so your valve stem seals
And knocking your tappet clearances awry.
No fruit of your driving: your plugs never dry,
Your tanks never wet – nor those of your daughters.
Trail a long lorry loaded with logs…

Speeding to get you nowhere, slowing down
To bring you neither calm nor safety.
Stones to puncture, sheep to stand stubborn
In your path. Dull bulls to dent your doors
As ever forking lanes confound your way.
May your turnings left end all at sea
Unless into quicksand; your rights into mines
Or else onto firing range. May you backfire
And blow the crook from the fist of St Pancras
To bring down all His curses on your neck.
Seven terriers to snarl at your inner tubes.
Rest at last in a black bog, whereupon
A slide of boulders to bury your wheels and you…

Crawl, you may as well, up your own silencer,
For be assured: you will come by no agony
But that you will survive to suffer it,
Your fate a mystery to your own people.

JOHN BIRTWHISTLE

The Next Poem

My next poem is quite short and it's about something most of you will recognize. It came out of an experience I had on holidays a couple of years ago. In fact, I'm pretty sure I'm correct in saying that it's the only poem I've ever managed to write during my holidays, if you could have called this a holiday – it bore all the hall-marks of an endurance test.

There's a reference in the poem to roller canaries, which become more or less mythical birds in the last line. I hope the context will make that clear. Incidentally, this poem has gone down extremely well in Swedish translation – which maybe reveals a bit about *me*! A word I'd better gloss is 'schizont'; if I can locate the slip of paper, I'll give you the dictionary definition. Yes, here we are: 'a cell formed from a trophozoite during the asexual stage of the life cycle of protozoans of the class *Sporozoa*'.

OK then, I'll read this and just two or three further sequences before I finish. By the way, I should perhaps explain that the title is in quotations. It's something I discovered in a book on early mosaics; I wanted to get across the idea of diversity and yet unity at the same time, especially with an oriental, as it were, orientation. And I need hardly tell this audience which of my fellow-poets is alluded to in the phrase 'dainty mountaineer' in the second section. Anyway, here it is. Oh, I nearly forgot to mention that the repetition of the word 'nowy' is deliberate. As I said, it's quite short. And you have to picture it set out on the page as five sonnet-length trape-zoids. Here's the poem.

DENNIS O'DRISCOLL

Toast

No lovelier city than all of this,
Cork city, your early morning kiss;
peeled oranges and white porcelain,
midsummer Sunday mists
that scatter before breakfast.

Mass bells are pealing in every district,
in the Latin quarter of St Luke's,
the butter *quartier* of Blackpool.
Each brass appeal calls to prayer
our scattered books and utensils,

the newly blessed who've put on clothes.
Why have I been as lucky as this?
to have found one so meticulous
in love, so diffident yet close
that the house is charged with kinetic peace.

Like a secret lover, I should bring
you bowls of fresh roses, knowing
that you would show them how to thrive.
Lucky it's Sunday, or I'd have
to raid the meter for spare shillings!

Or, maybe I should wash my filthy socks,
fret at the curtains, iron clothes,
like you after Sunday breakfast.
Normal things run deep, God knows,
like love in flat-land, eggs on toast.

THOMAS McCARTHY

The Tired Tourists

Too many dreams are attached to temples:
The beautiful water-colours we will do at sunset,
When the sunset never lasts long enough
And the cypresses run into the sky;
The wonderful poems we will write about temples,
Which become surfeited on description.
With a bit of luck though we will manage to lose
The guide-book which contains the glossary of terms,
And leave our best brushes on the small
Round table on a verandah we will never return to.

ANTHONY HOWELL

Aegean

I

Love
The network of islands
And the prow of its foam
And the gulls of its dreams
On its highest mast a sailor
Whistles a song.

Love
Its song
And the horizons of its voyage
And the sound of its longing
On its wettest rock the bride
Waits for a ship.

Love
Its ship
And the nonchalance of its winds
And the jib sail of its hope

On the lightest of its waves an island
Cradles the arrival.

II

Playthings, the waters
In their shadowy flow
Speak with their kisses about the dawn
That begins
Horizoning –

And the pigeons in their cave
Rustle their wings
Blue awakening in the source
Of day
Sun –

The northwest wind bestows the sail
To the sea
The hair's caress
In the insouciance of its dream
Dew-cool –

Waves in the light
Revive the eyes
Where life sails towards
The recognition
Life –

III

The surf a kiss on its caressed sand – Love
The gull bestows its blue liberty
To the horizon
Waves come and go
Foamy answer in the shell's ear.

Who carried away the blonde and sunburnt girl?
The sea-breeze with its transparent breath

Tilts dream's sail
Far out
Love murmurs its promise – Surf

ODYSSEUS ELYTIS
Edmund Keeley and Philip Sherrard

To the Most Beloved City

Venezia,
ring of streets,
calm choral voice
in the glitter of rocking water,
from all the sad and solitary
suns, I have but you,
from all the gloomy abysses.

Between the mirroring of shadows
and roseate faces
your high chime hovers, sparkling.

ALDO VIANELLO
Richard Burns

Venice in Winter

FOR GITTA IN BERLIN

The clouds obscure the island and the church
And the cold sea is streaked with grey like mud;
Dark cypresses (but not a single birch
As in Berlin), edge the Venetian flood.
Follow the Lido with your wind-swept eye –
Long needle of the land that threads the sea –

Where white gulls in the stormy distance, fly
Past lonely gardens and the last green tree.

You wouldn't think the citizens would dare
To venture out upon the streets below
With all this frosty dampness in the air;
But when night falls you'll see the scarlet glow
Of braziers roasting chestnuts near the Square,
And sweet potatoes in Sant'Angelo.

PETER RUSSELL   *Venice, 1965*

In Praise of New York

As we rise above it, row after row
Of lights reveal the incredible size
Of our loss. An ideal commonwealth
Would be no otherwise,
For we can no more legislate
Against the causes of unhappiness,
Such as death or impotence or times
When no one notices,
Than we can abolish the second law
Of thermodynamics, which states
That all energy, without exception, is wasted.
Still, under certain conditions
It is possible to move
To a slightly nicer
Neighborhood. Or if not,
Then at least there is usually someone
To talk to, or a library
That stays open till nine.
And any night you can see Times Square
Tremulous with its busloads
Of tourists who are seeing all of this
For the first and last time

Before they are flown
Back to the republic of Azerbaidzhan
On the shore of the Caspian,
Where for weeks they will dream of our faces
Drenched with an unbelievable light.

THOMAS M. DISCH

Looking Back: Iowa

A decent provision of hills, enough to feed
The eye's hunger for curves; of rivers, of rocky banks,
Of lakes and of woods, enough, just, to remind a farmer
That not all is edible, far as his eye can see,
Cattle and corn are not all, with rabbit, pheasant thrown in
As a bonus from what's beyond
His acres, his ken; but when a blizzard rips
Branches from sound oaks not his world alone
Is exposed: an opossum, uneaten, lies
Dead under snow. And above all, before and after
Blizzard, hard frost, that sky –
Larger, more generous even than land's extent
And luminous now, in November,
As I rise to it, leaving the ribbed fields.

MICHAEL HAMBURGER

The Valley

Once I was jealous of lovers.
Now I am jealous of things that outlast us
– the road between Route 28 and our house,
the bridge over the river,
a valley of second growth trees.

Under the birches, vines
the color of wolves survive a winter ten below,
while the unpicked apples turn black
and the picked fruit is red in the basket.
I am not sure that the hand of God
and the hand of man or woman ever touch,
even by chance.

STANLEY MOSS

In Your Mind

The other country, is it anticipated or half-remembered?
Its language is muffled by the rain which falls all afternoon
one autumn in England, and in your mind
you put aside your work and head for the airport
with a credit card and a warm coat you will leave
on the plane. The past fades like newsprint in the sun.

You know people there. Their faces are photographs
on the wrong side of your eyes. A beautiful boy
in the bar on the harbour serves you a drink – what? –
asks you if men could possibly land on the moon.
A moon like an orange drawn by a child. No.
Never. You watch it peel itself into the sea.

Sleep. The rasp of carpentry wakes you. On the wall,
a painting lost for thirty years renders the room yours.
Of course. You go to your job, right at the old hotel, left,
then left again. You love this job. Apt sounds
mark the passing of the hours. Seagulls. Bells. A flute
practising scales. You swap a coin for a fish on the way home.

Then suddenly you are lost but not lost, dawdling
on the blue bridge, watching six swans vanish
under your feet. The certainty of place turns on the lights

all over town, turns up the scent on the air. For a moment
you are there, in the other country, knowing its name.
And then a desk. A newspaper. A window. English rain.

CAROL ANN DUFFY

Background Noise

The wind scrambles and thunders over hills
with a voice far below what we can hear.
Whalesong, birdsongs boom and twitter.
Sea, air, everything's a chaos of signals
and even those we've named veer and fall
in pieces under our neat labels. Waves –
how to speak of the structure of waves
when all disperses and there's nothing fixed to tell?

Yet, following with eyes and ears half shut
to the babble, you might catch a hint
of what the geese hear, crossing in their loose skein.
Only a hint. The waves are breaking
just beyond our reach, in noise and narrow bands:
tales from the next ridge, or when the universe began.

PHILIP HOLMES

Guarnerius

She was prepared to believe
The fraudulent label – it was her father's violin.
But they said, 'You must learn the piano
First.' She crossed her fingers
In the name of Guarnerius. Guarnerius is in heaven.
No kin to the keyboard with its ready-made notes,

She reneged – they would impose
A kind of nunnery discipline.
She climbed instead the domestic Eiger face,
Doing the thousand things that have to be done.

W.G. SHEPHERD

Echo

I

Except as I speak she is silent. When I speak
She answers in no accent but my own,
Makes her reply true to the last word
Repeating nothing which I have not said.
I speak and she replies. Yet her reply
Lingers upon the word as if the word
Awoke a memory of speech, of how to speak,
Not as I spoke but as she might have spoken.
I speak and she replies. My word is changed.

II

I have said: 'Mere acoustics'. I have said:
'After the word the word resounds
'In accidental halls, chance corridors,
'Briefly incongruous or briefly apt.
'And thunder in the hills
'Is mere reverberation.
'A limp scourge drags the dust,
'A whip cracks empty air'.
I have whispered in galleries contrived for answer.

III

I speak and she replies, making my word her own,
As if I spoke in the darkness of her dream
With the tenuous memory of her speech –
Delaying Saturnia with mischievous chatter,

Calling, disconsolate, down forest paths;
The pool, the broken surface,
The smooth surface unbroken.
I speak and she replies as if we met
With a caress for which there are no fingers.

IV

Here let us meet. She has heard this before.
And spoken this, though no tongue
Touch the teeth, though no lips
Shape the sound,
No living breath give voice.

Keeper of many voices, she has heard
All flesh made sigh and stanza.

And now I speak.

There is my word.
There is the interposition of silence.
There is the tremor in a flesh unmade.

MATTHEW MEAD

In the Ring of Green Silence

The young woman in the flowered dress
has sleep in her blue eyes;
a face contemplates them
between enormous hands.

Abandoned to the ring
of green silence
I rest my hands on her head
whose gaze is lost in high trees.

ALDO VIANELLO
Richard Burns

The Tunnels

The poor bring us back
to the tunnels where they play
echoing before and after as we pass them:
strummers, fiddlers, the jagged
tenor, the old woman
with the hurdygurdy on her knees
dirty fingers at the frets, a fist
cranking the strings into a whine
as she lifts her face and points
her eyes with their scrubbed out pupils
at footsteps: the boy with the flute
a stick making music, no tune but turning
on the third and seventh notes of the scale
those pivots of our moving, playing on them
sudden woods and winds blowing themselves away
so blue he blows, echoes
before and after in the tunnels
where we began and, be sure, shall end.

KEITH BOSLEY

Fair in the Stars

The night open wide.

Spinning on the moon's axis,
God's carousel.

Far from the crowd
Sirius the poet
is sobbing.

Among the girl-stars
Ursa Major is dancing.

The cylinder of the breeze
spins over the treetops.

Dawn on the way,
and a little old star
sells snowy nougat.

The night open wide.

FEDERICO GARCÍA LORCA
Christopher Maurer

Music

The music was bringing me close to things.
She set an arch between me and them
and I could fall from far, from spheres
without breaking a limb,
wasting not one drop of power.

Like a magnet the music picked from me
the coppery feeling, the feeling of violet.

It lifted them up, like blades
of sprouting grass.

And watching, he could see
a coppery field, a field of violet
above which slowly unfolds
the nocturnal chain of pale-blue stars,
under which,
temple to temple
rib to rib,
our lives embraced.

NICHITA STĂNESCU
Peter Jay and Petru Popescu

Lady Harpsichord

This is the way I think of you:
Robin-song soft and sweet,
A breath of fresh air, and a handful or two
Of red and white seed.

JOE WINTER

The Container of the Uncontainable

GOOD FRIDAY

Bells like coins falling sound today all over the city
between each peal a new space opens
like a drop of water on the earth: the moment has come, raise me up.

GEORGE SEFERIS
Edmund Keeley and Philip Sherrard

To Music

Music: breathing of statues. Perhaps
stillness of pictures. You language where languages
end. You time
that stands perpendicular on the course of transient hearts.

Feelings for whom? O you the mutation
of feelings to what? –: to audible landscape.
You stranger: music. You heart-space
grown out of us. Innermost of us
that, rising above us, seeks the way out –
holy departure:
when what is inward surrounds us
as the most mastered distance, asthe other side of the air:
pure,
immense,
beyond habitation.

RAINER MARIA RILKE   *January 1918*
Michael Hamburger

'I'll sing you seven seas'

I'll sing you seven seas,
Green skull upon the shore.
What are their memories,
Green skull upon the shore?
Quick sand & dead sand,
False dawn & cold horizon
Ever opening, never closing,
All the wrong cards in one hand,
Which evermore shall be so.

SALLY PURCELL

Sunken Oboe

Delay your favour, grasping pain,
in this my hour
of desired abandon.

An oboe coldly syllables
delight of timeless leaves,
not mine, and forgets;

in me evening is falling;
it is waterset
on my grassy hands.

Wings flit in a limp sky
trembling; the heart migrates,
leaving me fallow,

and my days, rubble.

SALVATORE QUASIMODO
Jack Bevan

Requiem on Poros

The gods are being forgotten. And if we happened to
      remember Poseidon tonight
as we returned to the desolate shores of Kalavria,
it's because over here, in the sacred grove one July evening,
while oars gleamed in the moonlight and one could hear
the guitars of ivy-crowned young men in the rowboats,
here, in this pine-covered spot, Demosthenes took poison –
he, a stammerer, who struggled until he became the best orator
      of the Greeks,

and then, condemned by the Macedonians and the Athenians,
    learned, in the course of one night,
the most difficult, the greatest art of all: to be silent.

YANNIS RITSOS   *26 June 1969*
Edmund Keeley

The Talker

Silence attended his funeral after all.
After all that fuss,
the air is an immense and empty wave
as indifferent and light as old news.

They said that he talked to newspapers,
flooded the constituency with private details
while the Party wept.
He did not! But the secrets

that he filed in his heart,
the sweet and remembered, the bitter
and contemporary,
are sealed for good in his impartial grave.

THOMAS McCARTHY

Long Songs after Short Songs

Long songs have split the collar of my robe,
Short songs have cropped my whitening hair.
The king of Qin is nowhere to be seen,
So dawn and dusk fever burns in me.
I drink wine from a pitcher when I'm thirsty,

Cut millet from the dike-top when I'm hungry.
Chill and forlorn, I see May pass me by,
And suddenly a thousand leagues grow green.

Endless, the mountain peaks at night,
The bright moon seems to fall among the crags.
As I wander about, searching along the rocks,
Its light shines out beyond those towering peaks.
Because I cannot roam round with the moon,
My hair's grown white before I end my song.

LI HE
J.D. Frodsham

The Tree of Life

Blossomed tree stands up in Tamoanchan
we were created there, we came to be there
there, the thread of our lives was strung
by the force which all things live for.

That is how I work gold,
how I polish jade,

it is the grace of my song.

It is as though it were turquoise.

It spun us around
four times
there in Tamoanchan
for which all things live.

ANONYMOUS AZTEC
Edward Kissam

You and I

AFTER AN ANONYMOUS 13TH CENTURY HEBREW POEM

You are Jehovah, and I am a wanderer.
Who should have mercy on a wanderer
if not Jehovah? You create and I decay.
Who should have mercy on the decayed
if not the Creator? You are the Judge
and I the guilty. Who should have mercy
on the guilty if not the Judge? You are All
and I am a particle. Who should have mercy
on a particle if not the All?
You are the Living One and I am dead.
Who should have mercy on the dead if not
the Living One? You are the Painter and Potter
and I am clay. Who should have mercy on clay
if not the Painter and Potter? You are the Fire
and I am straw. Who should have mercy on straw
if not the Fire? You are the Listener
and I am the reader. Who should have mercy
on the reader if not the Listener? You
are the Beginning and I am what follows.
Who should have mercy on what follows
if not the Beginning? You are the End and I am
what follows. Who should have mercy
on what follows if not the End?

STANLEY MOSS

The Flight of the Sparrow

'My lord, although we cannot know
The mysteries of the afterlife
The span of time we spend on earth
Appears to me to be like this:

Imagine sitting in your hall
In winter, feasting with your chiefs
And counsellors – your faces glowing
From flames that crackle in the hearth.
Outside, the wintry night is lashed
By winds and driving rain and snow.
Suddenly a sparrow darts in
Through a door, flits across the hall
And flies out through another one.
Inside, cocooned in light and warmth
It can enjoy a moment's calm
Before it vanishes, rejoining
The freezing night from which it came.

Such is our journey through this life.
But as to what's in store for us
Beyond the doors of birth and death
We are completely in the dark.'

JAMES HARPUR

Psalm

No one moulds us again out of earth and clay,
no one conjures our dust.
No one.

Praised be your name, no one.
For your sake
we shall flower.
Towards
you.

A nothing
we were, are, shall
remain, flowering:

the nothing-, the
no one's rose.

With
our pistil soul-bright,
with our stamen heaven-ravaged,
our corolla red
with the crimson word which we sang
over, O over
the thorn.

PAUL CELAN
Michael Hamburger

The Magi

Toward world's end, through the bare
beginnings of winter, they are traveling again.
How many winters have we seen it happen,
watched the same sign come forward as they pass
cities sprung around this route their gold
engraved on the desert, and yet
held our peace, these
being the Wise, come to see at the accustomed hour
nothing changed: roofs, the barn
blazing in darkness, all they wish to see.

LOUISE GLÜCK

Meditation

I must prepare my death.
Many times I have felt
inconsolable pain

throb in the tree's root;
many times have watched
white scattered limbs
flower on the sea.
I have stalked a track
wet still with blood,
unravelling the maze
back to the ancient lair
where the beast licks his wound.
Now at last I know
from what open source
streams human love.

And as I touch that wound
shivering with a strange dread,
three women in black
sit beneath my window;
heads bent in the sun
they sew; sew in silence
shroud and cradle-shawl.

I must prepare my death
not once but many times
with quiet devotion as
women sew a shroud,
bird builds a nest
or man lights a fire
upon the midnight hearth –
I must feed the fire
with all that I have loved,
memories as old as sweet
as apples kept in a loft,
touch of a vanished hand
or water underground;
consuming all until
death itself is consumed:
only the dark remains
calling into the dark

as the womb calls to the child –
I must prepare my life.

PHILIP SHERRARD

'In a small patch of heaven'

In a small patch of heaven
I saw the sun unseam,
become two shining stars
and these had black beams.

They shine and serve
as the Venus stars:
at dawn the morning star,
the evening star at night.

Their shapes rimmed in gold,
a miracle is worked:
the dark becomes fair,
not the fair dark.

Rays that are the keys
to this sea's port
if ports become a sea
all gulfs and straits.

Eyes with no such mercy –
but yet they have, look!
The rays they don in mourning
for so many lives wrecked.

LUIS DE GÓNGORA
Michael Smith

A Carol

It is a winter sky.
I take a fist of stars –
A hundred if you please –
And seed dark vacancies.

They choose a hundred lands
To throb above.
Each land is cold and yet
Not closed to miracles.

A hundred miracles
Would strain credulity:
If man can love no more
Than once in a blue moon

A God loves his bad world
One time in history
At most, and pours his blood.
He'll come next time as fire.

But in a hundred lands
The shepherds leave their flocks
To seek a manger child
Following my stars.

And in a hundred Easts
The wise men pack their bags
And leave their palaces
And people to the snow.

Each manger's visited.
There's one beneath each star.
There is only one child,
One miracle. One star

Tells the truth and stays.
The others draw their line
And fall into the sea
With their false promises.

The sheep have strayed meanwhile.
The people die of cold.
The shepherds will not stop
Their scrabbling in the straw.

The wise men have not homed.
They wait upon the child
Although he died and rose
Too long ago for love
Except by miracle.

MICHAEL SCHMIDT

The Question

And so we too came where the rest have come,
To where each dreamed, each drew, the other home
From all distractions to the other's breast,
Where each had found, and was, the wild bird's nest.
For that we came, and knew that we must know
The thing we know of but we did not know.

We said then, What if this were now no more
Than a faint shade of what we dreamed before?
If love should here find little joy or none,
And done, it were as if it were not done;
Would we not love still? What if none can know
The thing we know of but we do not know?

For we know nothing but that, long ago,
We learnt to love God whom we cannot know.

I touch your eyelids that one day must close,
Your lips as perishable as a rose:
And say that all must fade, before we know
The thing we know of but we do not know.

F.T. PRINCE

The Dusts

(In Zen parlance, sight, sound, smell, taste, touch
and thought 'defile the pure mind'. The world which
we perceive like this is 'the realm of the six dusts'.)

I see you and a blur occurs
which I call love. The held you
vanishes. Lightly I interpret
gestures, smiles. You are
to me each absence
what I've never seen.

The flute
adds emptiness
to emptiness. And wet
chrysanthemums in autumn
touch the air.

A haze called
perception concealing
what?
    Golden
nothingness: jade–ash:
the mere
skeleton of the gods.

Radiance is where
sense is, you are.
Paucity of detour, of

withdrawal, the
recoiling from law.

Scattering the abstract
with questions like a blind man's
index. The nerves taut
as a finch pierces mist.
Bewilderment of
apples –
scarlet, tart –
in a curtained room.
Or the praise of
twilight circling the kiss.

Wine nor the grain of teak,
the silk you have
describing your skin;
sesame-seeds nor all
the magic of nakedness... Let's
think about that

HARRY GUEST

Golden Lines

So then – all things feel! – PYTHAGORAS

Do you believe that thought, free-thinking Man,
Is yours alone in this world that bursts with life?
Your liberty controls the powers you have,
But the universe is absent from your plan.

Respect in animals an active mind:
Each flower to Nature is a blossomed soul;
A mystery of love inhabits metal;
'All things feel!' And all sway humankind.

Beware the blind wall with its watchful gaze:
Tied to the heart of matter is a word...
Make matter serve no use that's impious!

Often a God lives in obscure things hid;
And like an eye at birth veiled by its lid,
Under the skin of stones a pure soul grows!

GÉRARD DE NERVAL
Peter Jay

Virgin Verses (1860)

O childhood memories – drinking milk at meals! –
And adolescence, high on high ideals!
When still a boy, imagining the scene
A woman offers, and to soothe the spleen
Of having a wet splinter of a cock
Capped with a great big foreskin where my stock
Of seed bubbles, a soapy source of fear –
I used to wank to the Platonic Idea
Of a nanny with a crotch of corduroy.

And ever since... caps off, for the same joy!

PAUL VERLAINE
Alistair Elliot

Paul Verlaine in Lincolnshire

I

For a while he had that famous friendship.
But what's inspired debauchery
and manic vision

to illuminations from the English hymnal?
Keble's stanzas? Wesley's? Stanzas
by good Bishop Ken?
Ô mon Dieu, vous m'avez blessé d'amour.

For indulgence, there was Tennyson.
He walked to Boston from the grammar school
in Stickney to confess.

II

And wrote *Sagesse* there in Lincolnshire.
And went to chapel,
and taught the ugly boys finesse.
He had been condemned to death,
he boasted, in the Siege
of Paris…
            Colonel Grantham and
the credulous headmaster
listened to the story
of his clever rescue by Thiers…

Even in the hands of Debussy, Fauré,
the Catholic *lied* Verlainian would sing
the strangest nonconformist airs.

Ô mon Dieu, vous m'avez blessé d'amour.

III

And to proper Mallarmé he wrote
about the absinthe: *I'd still take it
with sugar…*
The school record books
do not suggest
that he excelled at rugger.

O there were many rhymes –
But he was on his best behavior,
pious, calm, bourgeois.

The peaceful English countryside
acted on his conscience
like a rudder.

Ô mon Dieu, vous m'avez blessé d'amour.

JOHN MATTHIAS

Small Prayer without Pretensions

Our Father that was in Heaven... — PAUL BOURGET

Our Father who art in Heaven (oh, up there, Father,
Conception infinite of which we are not able!)
Give us this day our daily bread... Oh, we'd rather
You let us for a bit sit round Your Table.

Say, d'you take us for such wretched kids and trifling
From whom things serious must be hidden still?
And only Slaves can be admitted by *Thy Will*
On earth as it is in Heaven?... It's so stifling.

At least, though, by your smiling *lead us not* hereafter
Into temptation where we might embrace your heart!
Leave us in peace, to better worlds dead for a start,
To graze our patch and fornicate, and roar with laughter!

To graze our patch and fornicate, and roar with laughter!...

JULES LAFORGUE
Peter Dale

Prayer

Some days, although we cannot pray, a prayer
utters itself. So, a woman will lift
her head from the sieve of her hands and stare
at the minims sung by a tree, a sudden gift.

Some nights, although we are faithless, the truth
enters our hearts, that small familiar pain;
then a man will stand stock-still, hearing his youth
in the distant Latin chanting of a train.

Pray for us now. Grade I piano scales
console the lodger looking out across
a Midlands town. Then dusk, and someone calls
a child's name as though they named their loss.

Darkness outside. Inside, the radio's prayer –
Rockall. Malin. Dogger. Finisterre.

CAROL ANN DUFFY

Grace Before Liberty

Compassionate one, at edge of water,
reeling shoals that leap to your line:
each fish's head not yet stone-beaten
is another of your generous deeds.

For it is gentle, gentle release
into your keep-net that keeps till sunset
and easy the dance in fading hours,
the flicker round silk precincts of vanity.

Then count the score, hurt not a scale,
return us to swim free as water:
think lightly we go to eat at weed,
to sperm, to be fished again.

But I have swallowed your barb too deep,
hooked with a gilt-crystal hook:
seeping away, the long dark fin
unravels to mist staining your stream.

JOHN BIRTWHISTLE

Daunia

from THE ELEGIES OF QUINTILIUS

Generous wick with the oil of the coconut palm
Kindling each evening our own nuptial flame,
Witness you were of the love-act a number of times
Nightly, in the city of Sfax in my youthful days,
Till Daunia left me to shiver in an empty bed.
She it was who originally insisted on this
Petting and kissing by lamplight till long after dawn
Made weak the once-upright flame at our bedside.
Possible outcomes or permanency never entered
Our heads that were full of sex-games and gladiators;
The arena by day and the dust of our bed by night
With the trim wick glowing, and the wail of musicians
On the other side of the forum, with flutes and a drum
Loading the evening air with voices and wine,
Kept us too busy for thoughts of a home or of infants.
Now she has left me, now she's run off with another
(Rotten scum of a fellow from Rome with more
Gold in his purse than ever my father had
Before the drachma crashed and the markets went dead), –
With him she's gone off, they leave on the next boat for Rome.
She knocked on my door in the morning to say goodbye

161

'Don't weep, Quintilius, you will soon find another nice girl
To warm you in bed and wash your hair before sleep.
You'll forget your sweet Daunia long before she
Ceases to long for a former lover in Sfax.'
I couldn't bear to hear more of these words, so quickly
Went out into the backyard with the chickens
And wept, leaving the rest of her message to fall
On the polished brass knocker, my father's pride.
I had often thought I was going to end up a failure;
At the worst I had thought 'This girl will be a good
Wife to me now I'm a failure at everything else
Unbraiding her hair in the evening and lulling our babes
To sleep as the sun goes down on our modest house',
But had never troubled to ask her. Now she has gone,
And the bright streets of Rome will claim her the rest
Of her girlish days. Perhaps I shall die single
Not troubling to cook myself breakfast or
Keep more than a few half-bottles in the house
Of cheap red wine, and a jar of black olives.
Delicacies cost such a lot –
Without her to want an occasional bracelet
I shall die with my palms clean of the dust of gold
And be none the worse off. 'O Mother Venus
What can your poor sons do deserted by girls
They have ever taken for granted? It hurts.
Send either another Greek courtesan
Who is tired of life in the brothels, and is seeking a home
Modest enough for dull me to provide for,
Or end this unnecessary slowness of days.
I'll make her a good husband I promise you;
Just find me a house with a field not too far from the city
With space enough for chickens, a cock, a pig and a cow:
Let it have three or four gnarled and split olive trees
With ripe berries in early November; let it
Have ample room for the winter-wheat and a terrace
Of large-leaved vines for the summer months.
And don't forget to remind your old father
To make sure there's rain when it's needed. Dear Goddess

I'd soon take root at the edge of the city of Sfax
Provided my new wife doesn't turn out a scold
And further invasions don't interrupt the quick-footed hours
With parties of homeless and hungry looking for food.'
What a fool I was not to ask that girl at the time:
Her soft fingers made sweet our evening food
And she never refused to delight in the joys of Love.
I doubt I shall find another, at least in this age.

PETER RUSSELL

Wulf

To *my* people it would be as if they were given a gift.
But will *they* welcome him,
                             if he comes among them?

    It is not so with us.

I wait upon one island,
                             Wulf on another
bound fast all round with fens,
where there dwell men intent upon murder.
Will they welcome him,
                             if he comes among them?

    It is not so with us.

Full of hope, with my Wulf,
I withstood far wanderings.
When it was rainy weather and I sat crying,
when the battle-shrewd man covered me with his arms,
it was such delight to me,
                             but it was also pain...

Wulf, my Wulf, my thoughts of you
and your seldom coming sicken me:
my heart mourns, having no hunger…

Do you hear, Eadwacer?
Wulf shall carry off our child to the woods…

It is easy to tear apart what was never joined –
the song of us two together.

ANONYMOUS OLD ENGLISH
Gavin Bantock

'Love in silence'

Love in silence shall
its levy of tears
draw from the eyes, ears
fill with clamour,

familiar impress
takes (already)
the heart,

darkness & light
powerless both
this charm to unwind:

Those wings, my Cupids
so strong in urging love
so weak now
at the time of separation.

MELEAGER
Peter Whigham

'Living / with her'

from LOVE POEMS OF THE VITH DALAI LAMA

Living
with her
in whom
my heart
is lost,

groping
beneath
the sleep
of ocean,
searching
the sea-bed
for the
pearl self-
formed in
boyhood

PETER WHIGHAM

'I saw the tracks of angels'

I saw the tracks of angels in the earth,
The beauty of heaven walking by itself on the world.
Joke or sorrow now, it seems a dream
Shadow, or smoke.

I saw a kind of rain that made the sun ashamed,
And heard her, speaking sad words, make mountains
Shift, the rivers stop.

Love, wisdom, valor, pity, pain,
Made better harmony with weeping
Than any other likely to be heard in the world.

And the air and the wind were so filled with this deep music
No single leaf moved on its still branch.

FRANCIS PETRARCH
Nicholas Kilmer

Small Cold Poem

All that night fell
splinters of ice,
wounding the gardens,
and our warm bodies clung together, greedy,
not heeding the cold.
But when we woke
I found my heart
stuck full of them and freezing
like a painted Baroque martyr.

SALLY PURCELL

Words, Wide Night

Somewhere on the other side of this wide night
and the distance between us, I am thinking of you.
The room is turning slowly away from the moon.

This is pleasurable. Or shall I cross that out and say
it is sad? In one of the tenses I singing
an impossible song of desire that you cannot hear.

La lala la. See? I close my eyes and imagine
the dark hills I would have to cross
to reach you. For I am in love with you and this

is what it is like or what it is like in words.

CAROL ANN DUFFY

Missing Persons

Just because I neither smiled nor spoke –
Letting you pass me with the saluting glance
Which any attractive woman can take as tribute –
Don't think that I didn't know you
Or that you – staring ahead,
Recognition in the corner of an eye –
Did not know me.

I was in love with you at the age of ten and kept silent.
Your hair was yellower then and longer,
You wore prettier dresses than most of the girls.
Either we share an excellent memory for faces
Or ghosts inhabit the flesh.

MATTHEW MEAD

The Small Change

The small change of love, the little coins –

a backward glance of the eye, a shopping note propped on
the hall table, a joke (unspoken) shared in company, even
a few words grunted at breakfast –

these are as necessary for the commerce of the heart

as the credit cards and banker's orders and overdrafts of passion

and like archaeologists we shall discover them where they have
   fallen, half buried in the silt of our affection, marked
   perhaps by the corrosion of time but soon repolished in
   memory,

irrefutable evidence, collectors' items, each with its date and
   face value, each with its weight and measure of
   perceptible happiness.

GAEL TURNBULL

Waiting for a Lover

He swore he would come at moonrise;
The moon has risen, but he doesn't come.
Probably where he lives, the mountains
Are high and the moon is slow to rise.

NŬNGUN
Kim Jong-gil

Sailing Away from Night
FOR SESKIN KELLY

I listen to a thrush
its clear notes
beheading a stranger
out there
in the distance
where you stand

168

feeding the afternoon
with the fruits
we have collected
from the wood
in which the moon sleeps
waiting for nightfall
like an assassin

when night returns
we become children again
afraid of the dark of sleep

and in the room
lit by lightning
I listen to your whispered words
painted with sleeplessness

in the darkness
we wait for the boat
to take us out of the night
the boat as light
and as blonde as your hair
sailing on the waves of our fears

JOHN DIGBY

She Passes Through the Poem
AGGIE

I did not own
even the gesture my hand was
made of, or the measure
of her shoulder through
the elegance of itself,
the bowed bone,
          the possession

of edict, the semiotic
placing of uncial
to its rightful line;
of letters and their shadows
and all the beauty
          of passage.

          I am beginning
to resemble those who have insisted
they do not stand in the field
my poems occupy.
          I do not know
this poem yet, for example,
or its rabid structure.
But at least I am not alone
in the abuses of thews
and flowers and music
which are there of their own
winding and all the paraphernalia
of speech and so on.

In light and darkness
and her sweet presences
which travel to us:
out of the forest
the boundaries
          the doors.

ASA BENVENISTE

Warming Her Pearls

Next to my own skin, her pearls. My mistress
bids me wear them, warm them, until evening
when I'll brush her hair. At six, I place them
round her cool, white throat. All day I think of her,

resting in the Yellow Room, contemplating silk
or taffeta, which gown tonight? She fans herself
whilst I work willingly, my slow heat entering
each pearl. Slack on my neck, her rope.

She's beautiful. I dream about her
in my attic bed; picture her dancing
with tall men, puzzled by my faint, persistent scent
beneath her French perfume, her milky stones.

I dust her shoulders with a rabbit's foot,
watch the soft blush seep through her skin
like an indolent sigh. In her looking-glass
my red lips part as though I want to speak.

Full moon. Her carriage brings her home. I see
her every movement in my head… Undressing,
taking off her jewels, her slim hand reaching
for the case, slipping naked into bed, the way

she always does… And I lie here awake,
knowing the pearls are cooling even now
in the room where my mistress sleeps. All night
I feel their absence and I burn.

CAROL ANN DUFFY

The Young Man of Galway's Lament

'As Mr Yeats puts it, the countryman's "dream
has never been entangled by reality."'
–LADY GREGORY, *Poets and Dreamers*, 1931

It was the first week of the falling year.
Your lips had touched the berries of the hedgerows
Leading from my home to the folded hills beyond;

The birds remembered the melodies
Your mouth would sweeten between reflective smiles;
Your absent breathing piled leaves against the wall
And raised the flames higher in the hearth.

You said once that before you would ever leave me
The Slievebloom Mountains would be worn away by wind
The Golden Vale of Tipperary would become as the Syrian desert
The sails of the Norseman would again unfurl the horizon
And snakes would dance a jig on Croagh Patrick's peak.

Your words deceived me, your eyes deepened my belief,
Your dimples were snares I fell headlong into
The pureness of your skin blinded me like snow
Your slender nape prolonged my innocence
And your kisses stole away the days of the week.

Winter brought you back to me.
Your sighs the north wind sent below my door
The stars shivered like the nerve tips of my spine
When the frosted gate-latch clinked and your footfall
Closed in on the top of my neck.
Every night the linen bedsheets tried to recall
The lolling heat and fragrance of your limbs.

You told me once I was the king of Munster
The king of Ulster, the king of Connacht
The king of Leinster, the high king of Tara
And that one thought of malice towards you
Would summon the feral armies of the Danes
The chain-mailed horses of the Norman knights
And the cold stare of the English men-at-arms.

The round towers of Ireland lie in ruin
Homesteads feed their stones to all the walls around them
The hermits have departed from the hills
The crows pick entrails from the broken roads
The rains boil the fields to slurry

But there never once took root in my breast
A single dark thought about you.

You played the goose with me, you dallied with me
You said the young men of Clare and Galway
At night when they lay with their women
All gazed on your face, your parted lips.
Your hair you said flashed the fire of a conquistador
Your cheekbones were fashioned in Córdoba
Your ankles were as fine as those of Queen Isabella.

When spring came it brought the memory of the spring before,
The morning we opened every door and window
And all the vapours smoking from the boglands
And all the vapours thinning down from clouds
Had suddenly vanished
And the colours of the hills and meadows were restored
In the gentle thaw of softened air.
There was rejoicing in the land
As if all the fiddle players from Cork to Donegal
Had opened windows to let their stringy music
Rise over trees and onward into river valleys
Over loughs and mountains into the breasts
Of every man, woman and child.

Summer will soon come upon the land.
It was the time you took yourself away
The time when wheat spilled over from the fields
The copper beeches flounced their heavy dresses
And the early sun blanched the stones of hilltop cairns.
Do you now dine at the table of a gentleman
And avert your eyes into a silver cup of wine?
Did you fall in with the tinkers of Leitrim or Fermanagh?
Or did you cross the ocean to the western isles
Where the salmon leap and the hazelnuts abound?

I will tell the sparrows to look for your blue dress
The winds will blow to me your spoor

The rivers will pass along your reflections
Churches will sound their bells if you should cross their
    thresholds;
At night the owls will spy the tracks and pathways
And the eyes of fish will break the surfaces of lakes.

You will hear my thoughts when I think of you at night.
When I read, your eyes will trace each word with mine
I will walk beside you as you walk
And rise with you from your bed.
I am before you, I am behind you
I am above you, I am below you
I am the rain that softens the ground you tread
The wind that parts the hair from your face
The sun that settles like a halo on your shoulders
And the moon that dims your shadow
Wherever like a shade you flit soundless
Over fairy mounds, through ancient woods
Beside the streams that gush from wounded mountains
Over bridges, past holy wells and crossroads
Through the height, width and depth of Ireland.

JAMES HARPUR

Ch'ang-kan Village Song

These bangs not yet reaching my eyes,
I played at our gate, picking flowers,

and you came on your horse of bamboo,
circling the well, tossing green plums.

We lived together here in Ch'ang-kan,
two little people without suspicions.

At fourteen, when I became your wife,
so timid and betrayed I never smiled,

I faced wall and shadow, eyes downcast.
A thousand pleas: I ignored them all.

At fifteen, my scowl began to soften.
I wanted us mingled as dust and ash,

and you always stood fast here for me,
no tower vigils awaiting your return.

At sixteen, you sailed far off to distant
Yen-yü Rock in Ch'ü-t'ang Gorge, fierce

June waters impossible, and howling
gibbons called out into the heavens.

At our gate, where you lingered long,
moss buried your tracks one by one,

deep green moss I can't sweep away.
And autumn's come early. Leaves fall.

It's September now. Butterflies appear
in the west garden. They fly in pairs,

and it hurts. I sit heart-stricken
at the bloom of youth in my old face.

Before you start back from out beyond
all those gorges, send a letter home.

I'm not saying I'd go far to meet you,
no further than Ch'ang-feng Sands.

LI PO
David Hinton

175

Alison

In the big-framed window she is wiping,
I see a view like guide-book pictures:
the place, its Abbey and antiquities.
This is not the day to view it. She shivers
as the rain falls steadily outside.

She is settling into marriage as the
winter settles into Bath. His clever
talk is not what she remembers. There
are noises where he hit her on the ear.

Free talk. Free love. Among the interference
she senses memories of sex, athletic,
like a comic muzak. Buzzes echo
a passionate frankness that went off key.

She is settling to marriage, accepting
with strange humour. She has wiped the glass
with patience. She wants to make it clean.

TIM DOOLEY

Bees in the Rafters

Here I struggle to make a stern diary of love,
Moved by the intimate guest in your womb.

There is a flutter at the centre
Of the sexual paradiso. *Have you felt life?*

Like a mouse stirring among the sheaves
Or rogue honey-bees in the rafters.

But it is something wholly good, the psychic gift
And, also, more like a movement in the heart.

Even the trees are attempting an essay on love
With their red quality-ink of October.

There is a gathering in of everything in
Julie's place because of the rampant summer.

Late bees, drunk with the falling temperature,
Carry their late resources to where we are.

It is easier to speak of death than love;
We're better at idolizing politics than sex.

But I wish to frame the autumn of one mother-to-be,
To make autumnal your summer-loving fertility.

There is a movement at the centre of our days,
Just as the long hot summer moved the country.

Cathy, rogue bees in the rafters, October stores,
Embody the new meaning of what was only words.

THOMAS McCARTHY

Surplus

You hoarded, all our married life.
'New things cost the earth', you'd say.
Now, I have a key without a door,
a box of nails, a tube of fixit,
two cobwebbed candles in a jam-jar,
and so much rope I could cheerfully enmesh
a time-tripped colony of dinosaur.

But of yourself, nothing.
New things cost the earth.
And you've enough of that.

GEOFFREY HOLLOWAY

Grand-Daughter

Jeanne squatting on the grass looked pensive,
a serious curve to her pink cheek.
I went up. – 'Anything you want?'
For I obey my grandchildren, observe them,
try all the time to grasp what's in their head.
And she replied 'Beasties.'
So I parted grass-blades, found an ant.
'There you are.' She was half-satisfied.
'No, beasties are big,' she told me.
                                 They dream
the huge. Seas lure them to the shore,
lull them with a harsh rhythm,
enticing them with shadow
and the monstrous flying of the wind.
They relish terror, need the marvellous.
I had no elephant handy and apologized.
'Won't something else do? Tell me, Jeanne.'
She raised a tiny finger at the sky.
'That,' she said. It was time for evening.
I saw the moon's great disc on the horizon.

VICTOR HUGO
Harry Guest

Joanna from Ravenna

1

A ship on the sea, a bird on the runway of wind,
Joanna between petals of gold
In the marshes, between rain, wind, sun,

Joanna, sister of the years and the towers
Heavy with wind, leaning into the mud;
Joanna, sister of the star returning
Over the gentle skin of melted snow,
Joanna, sister of the will-o'-the-wisp –

Joanna wrapped in the fish-scales of her gown,
With a smile smouldering among the gold
Amid the teeming of insects hard and shiny, buzzing
Green like the ring on her finger;
Her eyes are two immemorial midnight seas,
All their depth distilled into two droplets.

Joanna, a fixed star; and rain
Coming from the ocean to her window;
A star fettered with the tongue of death,
Joanna breathes, Joanna smiles.

2

A ship on the sea, lightning in the year,
A dam in the hills, the humming of a turbine;
Joanna, sister of time, glitters on.

These words remember her. This wind
Lashing the window with late winter snow
Last summer touched her eyes,
Lips and hand, and her emerald ring.
And now, as I write her name,
Joanna listens to the pen, glitters on.

Joanna between the petals of gold
With a smile smouldering like phosphor
Listens to the swell of the sea, the flash of a bird,
The turning of a turbine before the dam bursts,
And to these words which will touch her

With the fingers of my fire, after me.

IVAN V. LALIĆ
Francis R. Jones

The Unmatched Emperors

They fire in the dark, the unmatched emperors,
Their huge desires kissing the walls.
Mosaics crack in the heat of their soles,
Sheets going this way and that, stark ravage.
Their wrath strikes sideways, spins to a drop
In the ice-blue gaze of the lake, where irons hiss.

Proceed, you early damned, always victorious:
We are anxiously scanning your nitric track.
Only too glad to be broken, pawn-scattered,
We line the squares no trees are in,
Stretching our hands for papal absolution
And most of us flayed to the bone.

Thirty or forty horses would fail to emphasize
The speed with which sand is flung in our eyes.
We, the whips, curled in on ourselves,
Fingernails tearing at the soundboard of the guitar.
'Starting from fish-shaped Paumanok…'
The island picked as clean as a bone
And the stretched tents, sun-carrion, skinned.

Born before your time, glad in your rage,
Scarcely awake to the raw fact of day,
Your vizors slip from your faces white as clocks,
While gentle sea-creatures carry you outwards,
Out from this despised bed, this ceiling of nettles,
Blowing you out over the warm savannahs
To where Achilles, unstringing his bow with a sigh,
Stretches an affable hand in your direction.

MARCUS CUMBERLEGE

The Siege

When they went out of the city walls to surrender,
the enemy was nowhere to be seen. — POLYBIOS

The walled town on a lance-tip. Unseen army.
The wells clogged up and low clung the smoke.
The eagle of the standard, live, shot from the sky
has been our food for a while. We haven't choked.
Then, a wave of diseases. Bygone apparitions
more faithful to the hearth than we, still shot
arrows far from the battlements over the plains.
Nothing. Only a star – the body-wound of some god.
And late, the hour of treason struck. Our drawbridge
was lowered by pulleys. Cowards, their foreheads in the dust,
begging for pardon. No one; only the moon, like the ridge
of a ship, going by the moat on a wind's crest.
Then no one again… We'll be shedding tears of blood
until our seventh death; we'll be possessed
with a sickness of open doors and smashed
windows. No one's ever about. But we, we have surrendered.

ŞTEFAN AUG. DOINAŞ   *1965*
Peter Jay and Virgil Nemoianu

After the Battle

My father was a hero though his smile
was gentle and it chanced one evening while
attended by his best hussar, a man
of strength and courage, he rode out to scan
the field strewn with the dead on whom the night
was falling. Then he thought he heard a slight
sound in the shadows. There, abandoned by
the fleeing Spanish troops, a soldier, dry-
throated, pale, bleeding, crawled on the road's brink,
and more than half-dead cried again, 'A drink
for pity's sake!' My father took the flask
of brandy off his saddle, turned to ask
his aide to hand it over. Suddenly,
as soon as the hussar bent down to see
to him, the soldier, some kind of a Moor,
lifted the pistol he was clutching, swore
an oath, took rapid aim and fired straight at
my father so the bullet struck his hat
making his horse shy back, tossing its head.
'Go on. Give him a drink,' my father said.

VICTOR HUGO   *18 June 1850*
Harry Guest

FROM *Amorgos*

They say the mountains shiver and the fir trees are enraged
When night crunches up the pegs of the roof-tiles for familiars
    to enter in
When the swill of hell runs in the froth and trouble of winter
    streams
Or when the parted hair of the pepper tree becomes
    a spinning-top for the north wind.

Only the cattle of the Achaeans in the fat meadows of Thessaly
Graze thriving and strong in the everlasting sun that watches
    them
They eat green grass, leaves of poplar, parsley, drink clean
    water in the channels
They smell the sweat of the earth and later fall down heavily in
    the shade of the willow and sleep.

Reject the dead, said Heraclitus, and saw the sky turn pale
And saw two little cyclamens kissing in the dirt
And he too lay down to kiss his own dead body on the
    hospitable earth
As the wolf comes down from the woods to see the dog's
    carcass and to weep.
What is it to me, the drop that runs and glitters down your
    forehead?
I know the lightning has written his name on your lips
I know an eagle has built his nest in your eyes
But here on the wet bank there is only one road
Only one deceiving road and you must take it
You must dive down into blood before occasion overtakes you
And cross to the other side to rediscover your comrades
Flowers birds deer
To find another sea, another gentleness,
To seize the horses of Achilles by the reins
Instead of sitting dumb to quarrel with the river
To throw stones at the river like the mother of Kitsos.
Because you in your turn will have been ruined and your beauty
    will have grown old.
On the branches of a willow I see the shirt of your childhood
    hanging up to dry
Take the flag of life for a sheet to wind up death
And let your heart not bend
And let your tear not fall on this unrelenting earth
As the penguin's tear once fell in the frozen desert
Lamentation is useless
Everywhere life will be the same, with the flute of the serpents
    in the country of ghosts

With the song of the robbers in the spice groves
With the knife of a sorrow in the cheek of hope
With the grief of a springtime nestling in the heart of the
    young owl
It is enough if a plough is found and a sickle sharp in a happy hand
Enough if there should flower only
A little grain for festivals, a little wine for remembrance, a little
    water for the dust...

NIKOS GATSOS
Sally Purcell

Looping Above the West

1

Take-off. And climb. The sun
at your back, Atlas
without an earthly base, escape
into hazard, worthwhile illusion
A few optimistic stanzas
drummed on the copper woods
A fistful of engine-roar
emptied into the aquarium of mankind
The mortar-boards whipped from the heads
of the philosophers of decline – ecstasy!
Slender rocket into the last
deserts of freedom:
Drunk with the spinning horizon
Looping above the West.

2

To be I, without splintering skulls
To be I, without smashing-in ribs –
Space! The angry ardour of youth
purged in the tourney of air
in the strutting beat of three motors

through the ogling branch of crows
silver rivers as tinsel
at the edge of deliberate wings
rhythms of almost spiritual lust
arrowed at quivering cirrus and:
To be I, living my own hour –
Dream in the petrol fumes:
Embraced by the horizon
Looping above the West.

3

But startled red signals glow
on the watchful instrument panel
The hour hurtles away
The sun withers
in the yellow potato-field
A dead sky drips
on ramshackle sheds
Below in the bridal bed of hay
a servant-girl conceives
the new epoch, ephemeral lust
My time is blown away
– a little smoke in the wind:
Imprisoned by the horizon
Looping above the West.

HEINZ WINFRIED SABAIS
Ruth & Matthew Mead

The Dead Man

Bringing shadows back from the river, we saw him coming.
His clothes gave off a misty smell of willow.
He found a chair, he took a spoon of quince
and stared at the dark corner with the cricket.

Someone took the lamp and shone it on his face.
He smiled quietly, wanting to be loved like a weak child.
He was grassy, blue-green and fumbling, say looking for his glasses,
a lizard ran out of his ear and hid in his white hairs.

His indefinite face went now to light now to darkness.
It was risky, he told us. As he walked he was always falling in a
    deep well.
Then he got up, walked downstairs and as he went to pat the dog,
it snarled and bit him and ran outside howling.

GEORGE PAVLOPOULOS
Peter Levi

'Against this'

Against this there is no poem then.
Big mountainsides where the small sheep are creeping,
mosswater weeping,
will see the end of Christ and his brethren.

The last trumpet: it is guerrilla war,
the one-eyed helicopters have gone hunting,
the deer are drunken
and I am drunk on the light breath of this star.

God changes what humans are conscious of,
we are old children, glass is our essence,
we give acceptance,
we know prisons, we are conscious of love.

PETER LEVI

On the Back of a Photograph

Hunched I make my way, uncertainly.
The other hand is only three years old.
An eighty-year-old hand and a three-year-old.
We hold each other. We hold each other tight.

JÁNOS PILINSZKY
Peter Jay

Night Patrol

What is there on a deep night in August
That conspires to lay a simple trap
Of moonlight, an empty road, a forest?
Why must a soldier guard his moving thought
Against conceit or against emptying
Into the imagined a last bullet?

The heavy insects knock against the wood
Of his gun as though in the instrument
Of death there is always a hidden light.
Behind a thicket the nocturnal beast
Drinks from its own shadowy reflection,
Its nostrils quivering at the coolness.

At each step he takes the soldier creates
A pocket of sound, a barren crater
Into which dust, pebble and stone spill back
As if to say, *Who makes the silences?*
Who is architect to these silences,
To all silence, if not a silent god?

The beast lifts its shadow from the water.
Listens. A ripple spreads along its flank

And through the fabric of all that listens.
The smooth leaf parts company with the branch,
And the owl blinks. The bearer of the gun
Absorbs through his body a disturbed earth.

MARIUS KOCIEJOWSKI

THERE WAS EARTH INSIDE THEM, and
they dug.

They dug and they dug, so their day
went by for them, their night. And they did not praise God,
who, so they heard, wanted all this,
who, so they heard, knew all this.

They dug and heard nothing more;
they did not grow wise, invented no song,
thought up for themselves no language.
They dug.

There came a stillness, and there came a storm,
and all the oceans came.
I dig, you dig, and the worm digs too,
and that singing out there says: They dig.

O one, o none, o no one, o you:
Where did the way lead when it led nowhere?
O you dig and I dig, and I dig towards you,
and on our finger the ring awakes.

PAUL CELAN
Michael Hamburger

Green, Green is El Aghir

Sprawled on the crates and sacks in the rear of the truck,
I was gummy-mouthed from the sun and the dust of the track,
And the two Arab soldiers I'd taken on as hitch-hikers
At a torrid petrol-dump, had been there on their hunkers
Since early morning. I said, in a kind of French
'On m'a dit, qu'il y a une belle source d'eau fraîche,
Plus loin, à El Aghir'...

                  It was eighty more kilometres
Until round a corner we heard a splashing of waters,
And there, in a green, dark street, was a fountain with two faces
Discharging both ways, from full-throated faucets
Into basins, thence into troughs and thence into brooks.
Our negro corporal driver slammed his brakes,
And we yelped and leapt from the truck and went at the double
To fill our bidons and bottles and drink and dabble.
Then, swollen with water, we went to an inn for wine.
The Arabs came, too, though their faith might have stood
     between.
'After all,' they said, 'it's a boisson,' without contrition.

Green, green is El Aghir. It has a railway-station,
And the wealth of its soil has borne many another fruit,
A mairie, a school and an elegant Salle de Fêtes.
Such blessings, as I remarked, in effect, to the waiter,
Are added unto them that have plenty of water.

NORMAN CAMERON

On the Wall of a KZ-Lager

Where you have fallen, you stay.
In the whole universe, this is your place.

Just this single spot.
But you have made this yours utterly.

The countryside evades you.
House, mill, poplar,
each thing strives to be free of you
as if it were mutating in nothingness.

But now it is you who stay.
Did we blind you? You continue to watch us.
Did we rob you? You enriched yourself.
Speechless, speechless, you testify against us.

JÁNOS PILINSZKY
János Csokits and Ted Hughes

Elegy, *19–*

So their killings became a subtle process,
politic; the masters of silence, bone, ash.
So the barley swells with the summer; hazes
    stall in the heavy,

quivering air. – *The ritual is necessary;
it has been with us   always*. Such accomplished
men, decisions glide from their fingers, every
    question is answered.

This is good; a harvest. And if so many
died, I was born after that… O why do they
visit me? their stains in the neutral fields, the
    weather their requiem.

PHILIP HOLMES

A New Thing Breathing

Rough and ready sea for the shoving on of ships,
tumble and rough waves, slow, see-saw ocean;
tough, tugging bitch with vicious voice
snatching at sirens' long locks and otherwise long lost songs;
hoarse virgin, purest of all whores,
unsated dustbin of sundry lands, spittoon,
eager coffin of sea-dogs and the dead at sea –

Demanding nothing of us but us sometimes and recognition,
taking willingly anything we care or care not to give:
keel-weary treasure-ships, or random
child-thrown coins or the whistle for wind;
I somehow know your welcome and endless cold-shouldering
and superficial smile in fair weather;
knowing though that under that there's no loving heart:
only the first cold womb, constantly weaning generations –

No man labours as you do for other dwellings to live in;
no pioneer wins so much at new shores;
you pass effortlessly over the highest peaks not once only,
leave bones of your bodies in the desert,
and the sound of your neuroses in ship-wrecked shells.

O my music-maker, when can I be with you again
and become, even from the most sunless places,
as a new thing breathing on the shining face of the world?

GAVIN BANTOCK

I Have Come Back

Sea, range of ruined rocks, lone land,
little houses packed in rows along the mirror
of the shining lagoon.

Green of the little fields, nets, dried seaweed and sails
in distant songs, you carefree men
who, as proud sailors, fall in love with every moon,
you women who, with flickering hands, embroider straw baskets
with silken threads, interlaced on fine carved wooden spindles,
I have come back to one of memory's smiles of the first green
    enchantment.

ALDO VIANELLO
Richard Burns

Lament

Voices, the wind
comes across
the bay, reedwork, Elsinore
sounded thus: over the straits
the coast, stretched
against the sky, there
on the headland stands
he who has called me,
Helios, broad-mouthed,
dark under the
eyebrows – the fires round him,
round shoulder and hair, the clanging
trains, uproarious: Planets,
the murderous
concentus of the world.

Over the bay,
far,
over the rain,
out of mists, shining with colours,

the rainbow – peace
is promised us.

JOHANNES BOBROWSKI
Ruth & Matthew Mead

Meeting

FOR JOHANNES BOBROWSKI

'Here I was born –
On the other side of the city,
Back in the murdered years;
Neither here nor there I'm at home,
On my way,
In search of the place.'

'Here I'm at home –
On the shore, I look eastward
Into the murdered years;
Where the lake recedes from sight,
And farther,
I come from there.'

And yet, we stand here together,
The water is quiet, our eyes
Fix on it, meet on it, rest –
On neither side of the city,
In a year that's alive.

MICHAEL HAMBURGER

Landscape Over Zero

it's hawk teaching song to swim
it's song tracing back to the first wind

we trade scraps of joy
enter family from different directions

it's a father confirming darkness
it's darkness leading to that lightning of the classics

a door of weeping slams shut
echoes chasing its cry

it's a pen blossoming in lost hope
it's a blossom resisting the inevitable route

it's love's gleam waking to
light up landscape over zero

BEI DAO
David Hinton with Yanbing Chen

'There is a gold light in certain old paintings'

I

There is a gold light in certain old paintings
That represents a diffusion of sunlight.
It is like happiness, when we are happy.
It comes from everywhere and from nowhere at once, this light,
    And the poor soldiers sprawled at the foot of the cross
    Share in its charity equally with the cross.

II

Orpheus hesitated beside the black river.
With so much to look forward to he looked back.
We think he sang then, but the song is lost.
At least he had seen once more the beloved back.
    I say the song went this way: *O prolong*
    Now the sorrow if that is all there is to prolong.

III

The world is very dusty, uncle. Let us work.
One day the sickness shall pass from the earth for good.
The orchard will bloom; someone will play the guitar.
Our work will be seen as strong and clean and good.
    And all that we suffered through having existed
    Shall be forgotten as though it had never existed.

DONALD JUSTICE

Joy

And Paradise does come

Paradise comes like a breeze and like a breeze
drifts elsewhere than where we are at the time

and we have no way of following the wind
to the world's end.

GAVIN BANTOCK

Laughter

We are light
as dandelion
parachutes we
land anywhere
take the shape
of wherever we
fall

we are often
the size of

grasshoppers in
a jungle of grass
or we're squirmy
chains of willow
catkins

then we become
curly seashells
knobby little
swimmers in a
sea of air
lying

on our backs
our eyes fly up
higher than kites
airplanes clouds
winds higher
than stars

we stare down
at the little
distant world
and we laugh
laugh laugh

MIRIAM WADDINGTON

Jittoku, Buddhist Mystic – 15th Century

Everything is blowing, his
skirts are blowing, he stands
hands clasped in enormous sleeves
behind his back, at his feet a
dropped broom. The strokes of the
broom made of dry sticks and the

swoop of a few live pine needles
shiver together, his unruly
chopped-off hair and the fringes
of his girdle all are blowing
eastward. Only the corners of his
mouth defy gravity. He is laughing,
humped against the wind with his bawdy
nostrils wide he is laughing: The
moon! Old boat of the white full moon!

JANE COOPER

Interlude of Joy

That whole morning we were full of joy,
my God, how full of joy.
First, stones leaves and flowers shone
then the sun
a huge sun all thorns and so high in the sky.
A nymph collected our cares and hung them on the trees
a forest of Judas trees.
Young cupids and satyrs played there and sang
and you could see rose-coloured limbs among the black laurels
flesh of little children.
The whole morning long we were full of joy;
the abyss a closed well
tapped by the tender hoof of a young faun.
Do you remember its laugh – how full of joy!
Then clouds rain and the wet earth,
you stopped laughing when you lay down in the hut
and opened your large eyes as you watched
the archangel practising with a fiery sword –
'Inexplicable,' you said, 'inexplicable.

I don't understand people:
no matter how much they play with colours
they all remain pitch-black.'

GEORGE SEFERIS
Edmund Keeley and Philip Sherrard

The Spaces of Hope

I have experienced the spaces of hope,
The spaces of a moderate mercy. Experienced
The places which suddenly set
Into a random form: a lilac garden,
A street in Florence, a morning room,
A sea smeared with silver before the storm,
Or a starless night lit only
By a book on the table. The spaces of hope
Are in time, not linked into
A system of miracles, nor into a unity;
They merely exist. As in Kanfanar,
At the station; wind in a wild vine
A quarter-century ago: one space of hope.
Another, set somewhere in the future,
Is already destroying the void around it,
Unclear but real. Probable.

In the spaces of hope light grows,
Free of charge, and voices are clearer,
Death has a beautiful shadow, the lilac blooms later,
But for that it looks like its first-ever flower.

IVAN V. LALIĆ
Francis R. Jones

Notes

1 Poems

Page 18: BEI DAO, 'A Picture'
Tiantian, the nickname given to the poet's daughter, is written in Chinese with two characters which look like a pair of windows. The same character also forms a part of the character for the word 'picture'.

Pages 120–121: from 'House / Casa'
Octavio Paz and Charles Tomlinson's paired sonnets are from their joint sequence on the themes of House and Day, *Airborn / Hijos del Aire*. The passages in italic are originally written in Spanish by Octavio Paz and translated by Charles Tomlinson; those in roman type, written in English by Tomlinson and translated by Paz.

Page 147: ANONYMOUS AZTEC, 'The Tree of Life'
Tamoanchan, also known as Tlalocan, is the mythical place of creation, 'the house from which we descend' where the souls of the dead also live as spirits.

Page 148: JAMES HARPUR, 'The Flight of the Sparrow'
The story is from Bede: *A History of the English Church and People*, II.13

Page 179: Ivan V. Lalić, 'Joanna from Ravenna'
In the mosaic of Theodora and her court in San Vitale, Ravenna, Joanna stands two places to the empress's left. The wife of the commander Belisarius, she was renowned as one of the most beautiful women of her time.

Pages 41, 72, 76, 165: The VIth Dalai Lama (1683–1706) was Ts'angs-dbyangs-rgya-mts'o, whose 62 love-songs are known throughout Tibet. Peter Whigham's poems are not translations but 'poems suggested by'.

2 Poets

FAGHANI was a 15th-century Persian poet from Shiraz.

JOHANN WOLFGANG VON GOETHE (1749–1832) is the supreme Romantic literary figure: playwright, poet, novelist, travel writer, art critic etc.

LUIS DE GÓNGORA (1561–1626), Spain's greatest poet of the Baroque period, was born and died in Córdoba.

FRIEDRICH HÖLDERLIN, the great neo-Hellenist of the Romantic period, lived from 1770 to 1843.

JULES LAFORGUE (Montevideo, 1860–Paris, 1887) is the poet whose influence on Eliot and Pound was so marked.

LI PO (701–762), TU FU (712–770) and LI HE (790–816) are the best-known poets of China's T'ang Dynasty. (Li He is more commonly transcribed as Li Ho; his last name is pronounced something like 'huh'.) Li Po's 'Jade-Staircase Grievance' and 'Ch'ang-kan Village Song' will be familiar to those who have read Ezra Pound's versions of the same poems in *Cathay*.

MARTIAL (40–104 AD), the greatest Roman epigrammatist, was born in Spain but lived mainly in Rome.

MELEAGER (*c.* 140–70 BC) was born in Gadara, educated in Tyre and spent his later life on Kos. A poet and popular philosopher, he compiled *The Garland*, the most important collection of ancient Greek epigrams.

GÉRARD DE NERVAL's sonnet cycle *Les Chimères* (*The Chimeras*) appeared in 1854. Born in 1808, he committed suicide in 1855.

NEZAHUALCOYOTL (1402–1472), king of Texcoco, was the most cele-brated of the Nahuatl-language poets and famed for his Solomon-like wisdom. The first and fourth syllables are stressed: *Ne*zahual*co*yotl.

NŬNGUN: a 19th-century Korean poet writing in Chinese.

The OLD ENGLISH poems are of uncertain date, probably 8th or 9th century AD. The riddle's 'answer' is given away by the preceding poem.

PALLADAS: a 4th-century AD Alexandrian schoolteacher and epi-grammatist, a pagan writing at a time of savage Christian persecution of pagans.

FRANCIS PETRARCH (Francesco Petrarca) lived from 1304 to 1374. He was a scholar, diplomat and poet, whose work greatly influenced the pioneering English poets Surrey and Wyatt.

QUINTILIUS ('one of the more shadowy figures of late Latin poetry') is PETER RUSSELL's fictional *alter ego*. His putative dates are 390–427 AD.

YI KI was another 19th-century Korean poet writing in Chinese.

Afterword

When poetry began to impress itself on me in my early teens, two anthologies were my source-books. The first is an old favourite, no doubt beside many bedsides other than my own: Lord Wavell's *Other Men's Flowers*, in which mostly old-fashioned, even by the standards of its time, poetry was linked by his personal commentary. For Wavell, poetry needed to be brave and declaimable: it was a soldier's companion in war and in peace. His taste was for the lyric and the narrative, as well as for light verse of the kind that is little written today. The thread that bound the book was his memory: at some time he had known all the poems by heart.

The second was Michael Roberts' *Faber Book of Modern Verse*, which first appeared in 1936, in its second edition revised by Anne Ridler in 1956. Here for the first time I encountered the mysterious landscapes of modern poetry: Yeats, Eliot, Pound and Stevens (I never did understand 'The Emperor of Ice Cream') beside poets such as H.D., Marianne Moore, Hart Crane, Herbert Read, George Barker, F.T. Prince and Charles Madge, whose poems mystified and enthralled me. It still seems to me the most satisfying and coherent collection of poets in the modernist (should I now say pre-post-modernist?) period, with an introduction by Roberts which compellingly defined the strategies of modernism.

At sixteen the taste for the exotic is strong. When I began to write, rebelliously of course, it was from the intoxication of the discovery of Pound's precepts and the example of the Beat generation: for a while Donald Allen's wonderfully anarchic miscellany *The New American Poetry* was my bible. Later I came to William Carlos Williams through Peter Whigham's advocacy in an early issue of *Agenda*, then Basil Bunting (re-discovered thanks to Stuart Montgomery's pioneering Fulcrum Press) with his marvellous combination of Poundian modernism and English solidity.

As a student starting to find my way through the thickets of contemporary poetry, I began to edit a small magazine, *New Measure*, out of which emerged the idea of Anvil Press. The first Anvil pamphlets and books appeared in 1968. One way and another my whole life since then has been bound up with this enterprise.

The sixties brought an explosion into print (and into live performance) of new poetry, British, American and translated, not only through small presses like Fulcrum and Asa Benveniste's Trigram Press but through Penguin's first series of Modern Poets and the Modern European Poets for which A. Alvarez was advisory editor. The Albert Hall spectacular of 1965 (Ginsberg, Voznesensky, Ferlinghetti, Corso etc. and a packed hall of 7,000) orchestrated by Michael Horovitz and others, was followed by the first Poetry International Festival in 1967, directed by Patrick Garland and Ted Hughes. It is hard to imagine that such a galaxy of visiting poets will ever be assembled again: Amichai, Auden, Bachmann, Berryman, Bonnefoy, Empson, Enzensberger, Ginsberg, Hecht, Kavanagh, McDiarmid, Neruda, Olson, Paz, Ungaretti... and in later years Popa, Pilinszky, Sexton and a host of others. I had the luck to work for the festival in that first and several subsequent years. Through it I met Nichita Stănescu of Romania and János Pilinszky of Hungary, poets to whom I became especially attached and whose work gave me my first close experience of translating contemporary poets. It is not too much to say that their impact on me decisively altered the direction of Anvil Press towards publishing contemporary poetry in translation.

Thirty years on, the landscape has changed. Specialist poetry publishing has become a tidal wave and a whole poetry business has developed, supported by the regional arts network and now aided by the lottery money which has helped put poets in residence in zoos, chip shops and high street stores.

In the sixties it was not so easy for a new poet to get published. Anvil was founded initially to do something about that. Nowadays the problem is not so much getting published as getting noticed among the sheer onslaught of printed matter. Some 2,000 books of poetry are now recorded as being published annually, about five times the quantity of 30 years ago. Print has become relatively a much cheaper medium. More may be neither better nor worse, it may be neither here nor there in the long run, but right now it certainly is *more*.

Likewise, modern poetry in translation was little published in any quantity until the Penguin series began, about the time that Daniel Weissbort and Ted Hughes started the excellent magazine *Modern Poetry in Translation* to introduce the most significant poets from abroad. But now translation is not selective or purposive enough. Foreign poets are often published not because they bring something different or new, but because of a hankering for the exotic, as a kind of literary travelogue, or sometimes for the frisson of vicarious danger with which poetry from parts of the world where political or social realities – repression, hunger, civil war – are more turbulent than ours can appease our sense of guilt for living in a relatively stable and comfortable country. Many of these translations are made without inspiration, without the necessity that drives strong art, even without due care, for documentary rather than fully literary purposes. There is a cultural industry supporting translation, especially from 'minority' languages, which takes it for granted than any translation of a poet deemed to be important is better than none. This puts the cart before the horse. Good translation happens when a poet works out of creative kinship or affinity with a writer, not when someone is given subsidy because this or that poet 'ought' to be translated.

II

There is a real public appetite for poetry but it cannot absorb the tendency towards over-production which has led to the present poetry mountain. The spirit of the age and of the arts bureaucracy is firmly set towards democratization and access. If this is at the expense of discrimination, it may now be time to insist that less is more.

I have always believed that poetry finds its readers, or readers find their poetry, by some kind of subterranean or osmotic process. Actually the whole of life works this way: we meet the people we meet, love the people we love and come across the art we need through chance and circumstance. Or if you prefer, through synchronicity, divine will or fate. But first the latent appetite for poetry is necessary, the appetite for language transmuted, language transcending the welter of words we deal with, deal by or deal through in our lives. That appetite can be awakened in many ways but it cannot be imposed.

There are committed poetry-readers, and to them a publisher can have nothing but gratitude: their support is the backbone of an enterprise such as this. But there are many people, among my friends too, who live without much poetry, and whose lives appear to be none the worse for this lack. It would be arrogant to maintain that poetry has an improving effect on its readers, as if it should be dispensed as a form of cultural medicine. It is only any use to those who discover that they need it, and neither 'society' nor education can be blamed for the fact that it is still a minority interest.

Still I have tried, without making any nods in the direction of the 'accessible', to make this a book which my non-poetry-reading friends might enjoy. In principle Anvil publishes poetry for whoever might come to need it. Perhaps those are the people for whom the poets write it. But a poet's prime allegiance is not to an unspecified, anonymous reader or to a public like an electorate: in the first instance it is to the possibility of the poem, the exploration of the common tongue. Only when the poet's work is done is there something for anybody, and for anyone who cares to come to it.

The job of publishers is to select, to present and promote the work of poets in the same spirit in which it is written. They also have to run a business which survives or falls by their success in selling books. Despite newspaper stories about a poetry boom which surface every couple of years, that has always been hard. Georg Rapp, who ran a poetry imprint in the late sixties, described poetry books as 'instant backlist'. This is mercifully not always the case, but in a highly competitive market books neither walk on to bookshop shelves nor off them without a lot of help.

Nevertheless I value both the distance and the intimacy of poetry, the complete directness and the discretion of its address. You can take it or leave it. It is non-invasive, which is a valuable quality in a largely invasive culture. It is as it is.

III

Many people want to know of a poem – especially a modern poem, which they may be preconditioned to assume will be difficult – first of all what it means, what it says. They would not ask the same question of a painting or a piece of music: but the medium of language raises the spectre of meaning. It is a truism that the essence of poetry is that it is unparaphraseable, that what it says or means is not what it does or is.

Another truism: there is content (subject-matter, subject: not quite the same) and form; when they are inseparable, good poetry happens. And a dictum of T.S. Eliot: 'There is good verse, bad verse and chaos'.

The poetry I find most captivating is that in which the play and the spell of words have primacy, as for example in the work of Derek Mahon and Geoffrey Hill. These are sometimes described as the musical qualities of poetry. They are at the interface between language and meaning; they are what the reader is most likely to hold on to first.

The relations good poets have with language and the ways in which they want it to mediate their ideas take so many forms that it is hard not to be a pluralist in poetry. Which is not to say a relativist. This book runs the gamut from the jokiest epigrams to the most serious examination of human turmoil. Poetry takes as many shapes and forms as poets need to find, and ours is a searching age. But also a deeply unfocused one. And much of the poetry that is written and published today is unfocused. It is formless, despite seemingly shapely presentation, tone-deaf in its insensitivity to rhythmic nuance, superficial in its propensity towards disturbing subject-matter, as if unsettling the reader were a worthwhile goal in itself. Sometimes it is driven by self-importance and has all the moral vigour of a style advertisement. But poetry is not alone in this.

Increasingly things have to sell and sell quickly. Yet the value of poetry is that it does its real work nowhere near the marketplace. Very likely it is harder now for poetry to remain true to its purposes when the pressures are all towards instant gratification. The professionalization of poetry and the sirens of the arts industry are not going to produce better poets, though they will produce more printed matter and more, better-paid alternatives to poetry, more dilutions of it.

Of all the possible responses to bad poetry, Gavin Ewart's in his epigram 'T. Sturge Moore' strikes me as one of the sanest. Of course the poem, though very funny, is unkind; it was not the poet's fault that 'Sturge' is such a fine portmanteau of *turgid* and *stodge*. I find the poem cheering: it comes to mind every time I retreat from a book of poems and can remember nothing. Dullness, pretension and bombast have always been with us, and after all bad poetry is not a criminal offence. Much of today's is worthy, and in a way not unintelligent too. One typical kind is the loose lyric, shaped perhaps in three- or four-line 'stanzas', which cranks everything up towards the final line, the rapt epiphany, the image that gift-wraps the poem, inviting assent and admiration.

If poetry is to be more than another entertainment, another branch of the performing arts competing for attention with the whole array of arts-related leisure activities which our culture deems to be necessary, it must assert itself positively and stand firm on its particular ground. Only then has it a chance of extending its territory in ways such as Tony Harrison has done with his work for television. But that comes about as the result of a particular poet's work and talent. However much one might want to see good poets more widely appreciated, or even simply given occasional chances to shine in performance, the poetry that is likely to cut a dash in the press or in performance is frequently imitative and watered-down. Its perceived merit of accessibility, that buzzword of artspeak, gives it a specious and temporary prominence which should fool nobody. The qualities that have always contributed to good poetry will continue to do so. Imagination is unprescribable and unquantifiable. The moral quality of honesty is still relevant and it is concomitant with the quality of accuracy or precision which informs good poetry: the right words in the right order. And poets should reject too easy alliances with anything.

It would be too grandiloquent to say that we look to poetry for revelation. It is not a substitute for religion. Nor does one turn to poetry for social analysis, economic advice, practical gardening or self-improvement tips, although it is possible one might find in some of it all these. We look to it for the thisness that it encapsulates, and the otherness that it evokes. We look to it for the broadening of our response, our inner experience.

In this sense poetry can quicken the spirit, enliven the mind, increase understanding. A good poem is, in different ways, part reassuring to its reader, part challenging. It reassures by inviting the reader's complicity through the intimacy of its address, it challenges by offering its own perspectives and perception.

But a poet must strive to avoid repetition. As a publisher, as a reader, it is easy to become bored by the near-formulaic approach which is so seductive, when a poet has settled into his own voice as into a warm pair of slippers. Such poets – and they include some good ones – strive less for the new than for the familiar timbre of their voice. Their poems become, in quantity, less necessary.

The story of twentieth-century poetry is partly that of the subversion of reason. The old divisions between 'raw' and 'cooked' poetry, or between the 'avant-garde' and 'academic', were based on this. The Romantic predilection for the irrational is still the norm, and the post-surrealist still finds a place in poetry, so much so that poets like Dick Davis can surprise one uncomfortably with their resolutely reason-based approach. Of course his lyric poetry works by subtle intimation, not by rational argument – that is a weapon for use in satire – but there are people who have discounted his work, largely because they have decided that rhymed metrical verse is *passé*, or that it is emotionally cold. They misjudge the reasonable surface. Or they simply want their poetic satisfaction too quickly, when it yields itself in slow phases.

If poetry works by intimation or adumbration, by conveying the implicit, how is it that some explicit, almost prosaic poetry has such force? Its values are those of personal rhythm and honesty. Personal rhythm is something developed and earned, not something innate; and the same may well be true of the honesty that is required in the making of a good poem, that rejects easy effects, that refuses to repeat itself or to fall into a well-worn practised pattern.

Poetry is not poetry until it is absorbed, it is not what you read but what you re-read. Poetry in translation works the same way; it needs to be as scrupulous and as inspired. Poetry – one might say art in general – is nothing if it does not bring the reader to thoughtfulness. A poem should stop you and create the space in which it makes you respond, think or ponder, be drawn in and then drawn out. Responses of many kinds may be invited by poems; but first comes immersion, then engagement, and then the joy of enjoyment.

IV

When I decided that thirty years of publishing should be marked with an anthology, I was not immediately clear what shape it should take. But I was certain that I did not want to produce a rollcall with sample work by most or all of the poets I have published. I wanted to give poems rather than poets primacy, and to choose poems which I personally like or value highly, not those which might be considered most representative of the poet. I wanted to create a portrait through poems of the values which good poetry can embody.

Of course there is a special pleasure in reading whole poets; a body of work is more than the sum of its parts. It forms its own poetry, has its own economy. But even the greatest poets are part of the continuum of living poetry; their work is not written or read at any other poet's expense; it can stand beside that of others without diminution.

Selections such as this cannot possibly do justice to the range and variety of a poet. Complex poets and those whose best work is in longer poems, such as F.T. Prince, Yannis Ritsos, Sándor Weöres or John Matthias to name only a few, suffer especially. As does Vasko Popa, whose work is almost entirely composed in sequences, and the sequences within cycles, the cycles within books.

I could not find any sensible way to extract from such long poems or sequences as Richard Burns' *Avebury*, Michael Hamburger's *Variations* or *Late*, Odysseus Elytis's *The Axion Esti*, Peter Levi's *Goodbye to the Art of Poetry* or his verse sermons. I would like to have printed entire Peter Whigham's 'The Ingathering of Love' and Sándor Weöres's 'The Lost Parasol' in Edwin Morgan's version. Similarly I decided against including a canto from Peter Dale's version of Dante's *Divine Comedy* merely for the sake of representation.

Oddly enough, I also found selection from Dick Davis's delightful anthology of medieval Persian epigrams *Borrowed Ware* almost impossible; the cumulative effect of the epigrams, the sense the book describes of a society (and a very different one from what one might expect) is so much part of its pleasure.

Overall I have followed my instincts in choosing poems which I thought would combine well in the general spirit of the collection. Finally I shall beg my reader's indulgence by mentioning briefly two poets, both alas now dead, whose work has been exemplary for me and who embody the purpose of the enterprise. Their poetry links present and past in a profound way; it is high-spirited, plays with language, takes risks, is dynamic – and finally beautiful. They are Peter Whigham and, through Francis Jones' versions, Ivan V. Lalić.

It never occurred to me that this book should have a title from any other poet than Lalić. Though a Serb, he considered himself a Mediterranean poet: you can sense his affinity with Greeks such as Seferis and even Italians such as Quasimodo. I wish I could have made room for some of his Byzantium poems. He was an Anglophile who translated Marlowe's *Tamburlaine* and knew a great deal of English verse and songs by heart; he even composed some spirited limericks in English, of which the best rhymes 'phallic' with the usual mispronunciation of his surname (Lalick: it is actually Lalitch).

Then Peter Whigham, whose Penguin *The Poems of Catullus* – idiosyncratic, mercurial, erratic, mostly brilliant – is a book everyone should read. Though his work may be flawed and inconsistent, he is one of those poets whose every poem, when it arrived, brought a sense of magical occasion.

We should not settle for less than that necessary magic. It is a quality of attention: the ability to modulate rhythm, to synchronize the speaking and the singing voice, to make verbal and intellectual music from the dance and play of words.

v

I cannot here thank adequately even a proportion of those whose good-will towards and practical services for Anvil have helped sustain it. To begin at the beginning, The Rockefeller Foundation, unwittingly perhaps, enabled the first few books with a grant to me in 1968 for 'creative activities'. Successive directors and staff of the Arts Council's Literature Department have aided Anvil with grants and with friendly and supportive guidance since 1969 : the late Eric Walter White, Charles Osborne, Kate Marsh, Josephine Falk, Dr Alastair Niven, Gary McKeone and Clarissa Luard. I am indebted to them all for their belief, kindness and understanding.

To Alison Wade, the late Rex Collings, Pamela Clunies-Ross, my long-time assistant Julia Sterland, Dieter Pevsner, Wite Carp, Eddy Buckley, Bill Swainson and Stanley Moss my thanks for long-term support, counsel and encouragement.

The late Asa Benveniste, who printed several early Anvil books at Trigram Press and designed covers for us, taught me whatever I learned about typography and book design. A glass of Bell's to his shade.

Successive managers of National Westminster Bank's Greenwich branch, Laurie Dennington, Joe Arscott and Wayne Parker, have tolerated our overdrafts and advised with good humour and experienced understanding of the problems peculiar to small businesses.

Many people have worked for Anvil in various capacities at various times: Patrick Dillon, Katy Emck, Graham Fawcett, Richard Hallward, Alice Harker, Nicole Lee, Margitt Lehbert, Caroline Lewis, Andrew McAllister, David McDuff, Ronni Mayell, Carol O'Brien, Josephine Pletts, Caroline Root, Jayne Ryle, Lori Sauer, Jacqueline Simms, Alison Smith, John Latimer Smith, Iain Stewart, Penny Taylor, Kit Yee Wong. To all of them my thanks, as to Bryan Williamson who typeset many books, and our recent cover designers, Richard Hollis, Tamasin Cole and Philip Lewis.

We owe much to our patient and skilful printers: Todmorden's Arc & Throstle Press, Alden Press in Oxford, Cromwell Press and Redwood Books of Trowbridge. Also to our distributors in recent years, Clipper Distribution and Littlehampton Book Services in the UK and Dufour Editions in the USA.

Finally, great gratitude to our sales reps, among them Philip Spender in the early days, David Parrish, Alice Caswell and others of Password, and latterly Rob Richardson, Leandra Holder, Pauline Clarke and Steve Powell of Signature in Manchester.

PETER JAY

Bibliography

ANVIL PRESS POETRY PUBLICATIONS 1969–1998

* indicates a bilingual edition

I Poetry in English: British and Irish

BANTOCK, GAVIN: *Anhaga*, 1972
– *Dragons*, 1979
– *Eirenikon*, 1972
– *Juggernaut*, 1968
– *A New Thing Breathing*, 1969
BENVENISTE, ASA: *Throw Out the Lifeline / Lay Out the Corse*, 1983
BIRTWHISTLE, JOHN: *The Conversion to Oil of the Lots Road London Transport Power Station and other poems*, 1972
– *Our Worst Suspicions*, 1985
– *A Selection of Poems*, 1989
– *Tidal Models*, 1980
BOSLEY, KEITH: *A Chiltern Hundred*, 1987
– *Stations*, 1979
BOTTRALL, RONALD: *Poems 1955–1973*, 1974
BUCK, HEATHER: *At the Window*, 1982
– *Psyche Unbound*, 1995
– *The Sign of the Water Bearer*, 1987
– *Waiting for the Ferry*, 1998
BURNS, RICHARD: *Avebury*, 1972
CAMERON, NORMAN: *Collected Poems and Selected Translations*, 1990
CONNOR, TONY: *Metamorphic Adventures*, 1996
– *New and Selected Poems*, 1982
– *Spirits of the Place*, 1986
CUMBERLEGE, MARCUS: *Firelines*, 1977
– *Oases*, 1968
– *Running Towards a New Life*, 1972
DALE, PETER: *Edge to Edge*, 1996
DAVIS, DICK: *The Covenant*, 1984
– *Devices and Desires*, 1989
– *In the Distance*, 1975
– *Seeing the World*, 1980

– Touchwood, 1996

DIGBY, JOHN: *Sailing Away from Night*, 1978
– The Structure of Bifocal Distance, 1974
– To Amuse a Shrinking Sun, 1985

DOOLEY, TIM: *The Interrupted Dream*, 1985

DUFFY, CAROL ANN: *Carol Ann Duffy: The Pamphlet*, 1998
– Mean Time, 1993; new ed. 1998
– The Other Country, 1990; new ed. 1998
– Selling Manhattan, 1987; new ed. 1997
– Standing Female Nude, 1985; new ed. 1998

EVANS, MARTINA: *All Alcoholics Are Charmers*, 1998

EWART, GAVIN: *All My Little Ones*, 1978
– More Little Ones, 1983

FULTON, ROBIN: *Fields of Focus*, 1982

GUEST, HARRY: *Arrangements*, 1968; pbk. ed. 1970
– Coming to Terms, 1994
– The Cutting-Room, 1970
– A House Against the Night, 1976
– Lost and Found, 1984

HAMBURGER, MICHAEL: *Collected Poems 1941–1994*, 1995; pbk. ed.
1998
– Late, 1997
– Roots in the Air, 1991

HARPUR, JAMES: *The Monk's Dream*, 1996
– A Vision of Comets, 1993

HARTNETT, D.W.: *A Signalled Love*, 1985

HEWLINGS, MICHAEL: *The Release*, 1972

HOLBROOK, DAVID: *Chance of a Lifetime*, 1978
– Selected Poems 1961–1978, 1980

HOLLOWAY, GEOFFREY: *All I Can Say*, 1978
– To Have Eyes, 1972

HOLMES, PHILIP: *The Green Road*, 1986
– A Place to Stand, 1977
– Three Sections of Poems, 1971

HOWELL, ANTHONY: *First Time in Japan*, 1995
– Howell's Law, 1990
– Notions of a Mirror, 1983
– Why I May Never See the Walls of China, 1986

KOCIEJOWSKI, MARIUS: *Doctor Honoris Causa*, 1993

LEVI, PETER: *Collected Poems 1955–1975*, 1976; new ed. 1984
– Death is a Pulpit, 1971
– The Echoing Green, 1983
– Five Ages, 1978
– Goodbye to the Art of Poetry, 1989

– *Self-Love*, 1983
– *Sun, Oak, Almond, I*, 1970
SHERRARD, PHILIP: *In the Sign of the Rainbow*, 1994
SILCOCK, RUTH: *Mrs. Carmichael*, 1987
– *A Wonderful View of the Sea*, 1996
STEWART, SUE: *Inventing the Fishes*, 1993
TOMLINSON, CHARLES / PAZ, OCTAVIO: *Airborn / Hijos del Aire*, 1981
TURNBULL, GAEL: *A Gathering of Poems*, 1983
WARD, DONALD: *Border Country*, 1981
WEISSBORT, DANIEL: *What Was All the Fuss About?*, 1998
WELCH, JOHN: *Out Walking*, 1984
WHIGHAM, PETER: *ASTAPOVO or What We Are To Do*, 1970
– *The Blue Winged Bee*, 1969
– *Things Common, Properly*, 1984
WINTER, JOE: *A Miracle and The Tree*, 1972

2   Poetry in English: North American

BRADLEY, SAM: *Manspell / Godspell*, 1975
CASSIAN, NINA: *Take My Word for It*, 1998
COOPER, JANE: *Scaffolding*, 1984
DISCH, THOMAS M.: *ABCDEFG HIJKLM NPOQRST UVWXYZ*,
    1981
GLÜCK, LOUISE: *Firstborn*, 1969
– *The House on Marshland*, 1976
JUSTICE, DONALD: *Orpheus Hesitated Beside the Black River*, 1998
– *Selected Poems*, 1980
– *The Sunset Maker*, 1987
KISSAM, EDWARD: *Jerusalem & The People*, 1972
– *The Sham Flyers*, 1969
MATTHIAS, JOHN: *Crossing*, 1979
– *Northern Summer*, 1984
– *Turns*, 1975
MOSS, STANLEY: *Asleep in the Garden*, 1998
– *The Intelligence of Clouds*, 1989
– *Skull of Adam*, 1979
– *The Wrong Angel*, 1969
PETERS, ROBERT: *Connections*, 1972
SHAW, ROBERT B.: *In Witness*, 1972
WADDINGTON, MIRIAM: *Dream Telescope*, 1972
– *Driving Home*, 1973

3 Poetry before 1900 in Translation

Individual poets

*BAUDELAIRE, CHARLES: *Volume I: The Complete Verse*, tr. Francis
  Scarfe (prose), 1986
– *Volume II: The Poems in Prose*, tr. Francis Scarfe, 1989
DANTE ALIGHIERI: *The Divine Comedy*, tr. Peter Dale, 1996
GOETHE, JOHANN VON: *Poems and Epigrams*, tr. Michael Hamburger,
  1984
– *Roman Elegies and other poems*, tr. Michael Hamburger, 1996
*GÓNGORA, LUIS DE: *Selected Shorter Poems*, tr. Michael Smith, 1995
*HÖLDERLIN, FRIEDRICH: *Poems and Fragments*, tr. Michael
  Hamburger, 1994
– *Selected Verse*, tr. Michael Hamburger (prose), 1986
*HUGO, VICTOR: *The Distance, The Shadows*, tr. Harry Guest, 1981
*LAFORGUE, JULES: *Poems of Jules Laforgue*, tr. Peter Dale, 1986; pbk.
  ed. 1987
LI HE: *Goddesses, Ghosts, and Demons*, tr. J.D. Frodsham, 1983
LI PO: *The Selected Poems of Li Po*, tr. David Hinton, 1998
*MARTIAL: *Letter to Juvenal*, tr. Peter Whigham, 1985
*MELEAGER: *The Poems of Meleager*, tr. Peter Whigham (verse), Peter Jay
  (prose), 1975
*NERVAL, GÉRARD DE: *The Chimeras*, tr. Peter Jay, essay by Richard
  Holmes, 1985
*NIETZSCHE, FRIEDRICH: *Dithyrambs of Dionysus*, 1984
PALLADAS: *Palladas: Poems*, tr. Tony Harrison, 1975; 2nd ed. 1984
PERSIUS: *The Satires of Persius*, tr. W.S. Merwin, 1981
PETRARCH, FRANCIS: *Songs and Sonnets from Laura's Lifetime*, tr.
  Nicholas Kilmer, 1980
*RIMBAUD, ARTHUR: *A Season in Hell and other poems*, tr. Norman
  Cameron, 1994
SAPPHO: *Sappho Through English Poetry*, ed. Peter Jay and Caroline
  Lewis, 1996
TU FU: *The Selected Poems of Tu Fu*, tr. David Hinton, 1990
*VERLAINE, PAUL: *Femmes / Hombres: Women / Men*, tr. Alistair Elliot,
  1979; pbk. ed. 1983

Anthologies

ALEXANDER, MICHAEL: *Old English Riddles*, 1980; revised ed. 1982
DAVIS, DICK: *Borrowed Ware*, Medieval Persian Epigrams, 1996
JAY, PETER: *The Song of Songs*, 1975; new ed. 1998

*JONG-GIL, KIM: *Slow Chrysanthemums*, Classical Korean Poems in
Chinese, 1987
KISSAM, EDWARD and SCHMIDT, MICHAEL: *Flower and Song*, Poems
of the Aztec Peoples, 1977; pbk. ed. 1983
POPA, VASKO (ed.): *The Golden Apple*, Serbo-Croat folk songs etc, ed. and
tr. Andrew Harvey and Anne Pennington, 1980
ROSSETTI, DANTE GABRIEL: *The Early Italian Poets*, ed. Sally Purcell,
1981

4   Twentieth-Century Poetry in Translation

Individual poets

*APOLLINAIRE, GUILLAUME: *Selected Poems*, tr. Oliver Bernard, 1986
BARTUŠEK, ANTONÍN: *The Aztec Calendar*, tr. Ewald Osers, 1975
BEI DAO: *The August Sleepwalker*, tr. Bonnie S. McDougall, 1989
* – *Forms of Distance*, tr. David Hinton, 1994
* – *Landscape Over Zero*, tr. David Hinton with Yanbing Chen, 1998
* – *Old Snow*, tr. Bonnie S. McDougall, 1992
BLANDIANA, ANA: *The Hour of Sand*, tr. Peter Jay and Anca
Cristofovici, 1990; 2nd ed. 1990
BOBROWSKI, JOHANNES: *From the Rivers*, tr. Ruth and Matthew Mead,
1975
– *Shadow Lands*, tr. Ruth and Matthew Mead, 1984
*BORCHERS, ELISABETH: *Fish Magic*, tr. Anneliese Wagner, 1989
CASSIAN, NINA: *Life Sentence*, ed. William Jay Smith, 1990; new ed.
1998
*CELAN, PAUL: *Poems of Paul Celan*, tr. Michael Hamburger, 1989; new
ed. 1995
DOINAŞ, ŞTEFAN AUG.: *Alibi & other poems*, tr. Peter Jay and Virgil
Nemoianu, 1975
ELYTIS, ODYSSEUS: *The Axion Esti*, tr. Edmund Keeley and George
Savidis, 1980
– *Selected Poems*, ed. Edmund Keeley and Philip Sherrard, 1981; pbk.
ed. 1991
FAVEREY, HANS: *Against the Forgetting*, tr. Francis R. Jones, 1994
*GATSOS, NIKOS: *Amorgos*, tr. Sally Purcell, 1998
HAUGE, OLAV H.: *Don't Give Me the Whole Truth*, tr. Robin Fulton and
James Greene with Siv Hennum, 1985
KIRSCH, SARAH: *Winter Music*, tr. Margitt Lehbert, 1994
LALIĆ, IVAN V.: *Fading Contact*, tr. Francis R. Jones, 1997
– *Last Quarter*, tr. Francis R. Jones, 1987
– *The Passionate Measure*, tr. Francis R. Jones, 1989

– *A Rusty Needle*, tr. Francis R. Jones, 1996
– *The Works of Love*, tr. Francis R. Jones, 1982
LORCA, FEDERICO GARCÍA: *A Season in Granada*, tr. Christopher
    Maurer, 1998
*NERUDA, PABLO: *The Captain's Verses*, tr. Brian Cole, 1994
PAVLOPOULOS, GEORGE: *The Cellar*, tr. Peter Levi, 1977
*PAZ, OCTAVIO and TOMLINSON, CHARLES: *Airborn / Hijos del Aire*,
    1981
PILINSZKY, JÁNOS: *Crater*, tr. Peter Jay, 1978
– *The Desert of Love*, tr. János Csokits and Ted Hughes, 1989
POPA, VASKO: *Collected Poems*, tr. Anne Pennington, revised and
    expanded by Francis R. Jones, 1997; pbk. ed. 1998
– *Earth Erect*, tr. Anne Pennington, 1973
QUASIMODO, SALVATORE: *Complete Poems*, tr. Jack Bevan, 1984
– *Debit and Credit*, tr. Jack Bevan, 1972
*RILKE, RAINER MARIA: *An Unofficial Rilke*, tr. Michael Hamburger,
    1982
RITSOS, YANNIS: *Exile and Return*, tr. Edmund Keeley, 1989
– *The Fourth Dimension*, tr. Peter Green and Beverly Bardsley, 1993
RÓŻEWICZ, TADEUSZ: *Conversation with the Prince*, tr. Adam
    Czerniawski, 1982
– *They Came to See a Poet*, tr. Adam Czerniawski, 1991
SABAIS, HEINZ WINFRIED: *Generation*, tr. Ruth and Matthew Mead,
    1968
– *The People and the Stones*, tr. Ruth and Matthew Mead, 1983
*SEFERIS, GEORGE: *Collected Poems*, tr. Edmund Keeley and Philip
    Sherrard, 1980; hbk. ed. 1987
– *Complete Poems*, tr. Edmund Keeley and Philip Sherrard, 1995
SERENI, VITTORIO: *Selected Poems*, tr. Peter Robinson and Marcus
    Perryman, 1990
STĂNESCU, NICHITA: *The Still Unborn About The Dead*, tr. Peter Jay
    and Petru Popescu, 1975
VIANELLO, ALDO: *Time of a Flower*, tr. Richard Burns, 1968
WEÖRES, SÁNDOR: *Eternal Moment*, ed. Miklós Vajda, 1987

Anthologies

MATTHIAS, JOHN: *Contemporary Swedish Poetry*, 1980
WEISSBORT, DANIEL: *The Poetry of Survival*, 1991

6   Other Anthologies, by editor

DUFFY, CAROL ANN: *Anvil New Poets 2*, 1995
DUNNE, SEÁN: *Poets of Munster*, 1985
FAWCETT, GRAHAM: *Anvil New Poets*, 1990
HOLMES, RICHARD: *Shelley on Love*, 1980; pbk. ed. 1983
SMITH, KEN and SWEENEY, MATTHEW: *Beyond Bedlam*, 1997
WATERMAN, ANDREW: *The Poetry of Chess*, 1982
WEISSBORT, DANIEL: *Poetry World 1*, 1986
– *Poetry World 2*, 1989

7   Fiction

GUEST, HARRY: *Days*, 1978
WHEWAY, JOHN: *The Green Table of Infinity*, 1972

8   Criticism and essays

HAMBURGER, MICHAEL: *The Truth of Poetry*, 1996
LEVI, PETER: *The Lamentation of the Dead*, 1984
– *The Noise Made by Poems*, 1977; 2nd ed. 1984

9   Limited edition pamphlets

BRODSKY, JOSEPH: *Verses on the Winter Campaign 1980*, 1981
COPE, WENDY: *Does She Like Word-Games?*, 1987
DUFFY, CAROL ANN: *William and the ex-Prime Minister*, 1992
HAMBURGER, MICHAEL: *Real Estate*, 1977
HARRISON, TONY: *Ten Sonnets from The School of Eloquence*, 1987
LOGUE, CHRISTOPHER: *Lucky Dust*, 1985
MAHON, DEREK: *A Kensington Notebook*, 1984
PLATH, SYLVIA: *Two Uncollected Poems*, 1980
PORTER, PETER: *The Animal Programme*, 1982
SPENDER, STEPHEN: *Recent Poems*, 1978

10   Miscellaneous

KISSAM, EDWARD: *Vietnamese Lessons*, leaflet, 1970
Twelve Poets, boxed set of booklets, 1972

Index of Poets and Translators

Index of Titles

Some Recent Poetry from Anvil